Making Agents Wealthy

MAKING AGENTS WEALTHY

The #1 Results-Oriented System for Women in Real Estate

Take your real estate sales to the next level without sounding salesy, chasing clients, cold calling, or door knocking

KAREN COFFEY

NEW YORK

LONDON • NASHVILLE • MELBOURNE • VANCOUVER

MAKING AGENTS WEALTHY

The #1 Results Oriented System for Women in Real Estate

© 2021 Karen Coffey

Published in New York, New York, by Morgan James Publishing. Morgan James is a trademark of Morgan James, LLC. www.MorganJamesPublishing.com

The contents of this book are not intended to be legal or finance advice in anyway. It is important that you do your due diligence and follow all local, state and federal laws, regulations and guidelines as each area is unique as far as real estate law is concerned. Always check with your broker to make sure you are in compliance.

ISBN 9781631952425 paperback
ISBN 9781631952432 eBook
Library of Congress Control Number: 2020939162

Cover Design by:
Megan Dillon
megan@creativeninjadesigns.com

Interior Design by:
Chris Treccani
www.3dogcreative.net

Morgan James is a proud partner of Habitat for Humanity Peninsula and Greater Williamsburg. Partners in building since 2006.

Get involved today! Visit
MorganJamesPublishing.com/giving-back

Contents

Introduction:

HER SECRET WEAPON

You are the designer of your destiny.
You are the author of your story.
—Lisa Nichols

Since 2009, I have helped thousands of women in real estate grow their business and be successful. In doing so, I've witnessed firsthand their daily struggle to achieve their goals while maintaining a positive work/life balance. I've coached them through their inability to pay their bills or handle the financial ups and downs of commission sales from month to month, and I've been a cheerleader as well as a shoulder to cry on. Through all the seminars, conferences, books, and on-the-job training, I've found that success as a real estate agent boils down to mastering three things: *mindset*, *skills*, and *systems*.

1. **Mindset** is the magic pill! Yes, you heard me right—there is a magic pill to getting everything you want out of your real estate career, and it's your mindset. I'm not talking about positive thinking. Having the right mindset is much more than that. I'm talking about a results-oriented approach to everything you do. In this book, I will take you step by step through what I call the Money Miracles and Breakthroughs Process. It will give you immediate traction in your business.

2. **Skills**. When you're skilled at making sales, you gain massive amounts of confidence. You close differently, you act differently, and your customers and clients notice. They know when you're skilled and experienced, and they know when you're bluffing. You have probably bluffed your way through a sale, so how do you gain massive amounts of confidence? In a word—skills! Effective skills will help you earn a lot of money in the real estate business. If this seems too basic, let's think about it for a minute. You've been to hundreds of trainings and classes, you've taken tons of notes, you know everything there is to know about the topic, and BAM! An opportunity comes your way to show off your newfound knowledge, and you feel like it's your first day learning to talk. You fumble over your words, you can't quite grasp what you're supposed to do or say, and with head hung low, you vow you'll do better next time. Knowledge has failed you, and the only way out is to get up, get into action, and get some skills. I'm talking about becoming a skilled master, a precision ninja, the Heisman trophy winner of lead conversion! This type of skill doesn't

happen overnight. I'll share some juicy tricks of the trade based on my own dreadful experiences and incompetence so you don't have to repeat my mistakes.

3. **Systems**. Systems make everything shine brighter, go faster, and run more smoothly. Having great systems to streamline your efficiency represents money in your pocket, but just any system won't do. You need systems that are liberating, effective, freeing, fun, smart, easy, plug-and-play systems that will make you a superstar. These kinds of systems are worth every minute of your time to implement, and produce a great return on investment. I will share with you some of my never-before revealed systems on how to make $100,000 in 100 days. This is exactly how I did it, even when I was in a new market where I had never sold real estate before. I did it all using effective systems. This is how my real estate clients are doing it month after month, and you can too.

So, get ready for a complete reboot of your real estate career. This is the secret weapon you've been hoping for. Grab a pen, a notebook, and maybe a latte, and get ready to learn how to outperform, outwit, and perhaps most importantly, outearn your competition, even if you're new to real estate sales or you've just moved to a new area and you're breaking into the housing market there. This information will uncover, chisel away, and rid you of everything that's been standing in your way of making $150,000, $250,000, or even half a million dollars per year in real estate sales.

Remember that magic pill I spoke of earlier? Well, the magic is about to start right now!

Making Agents Wealthy is *the* number-one resource for real estate professionals who are serious about growing their business and being successful year after year. More than that, this book is specifically written for women in real estate. It is meant to be read, studied, and implemented one chapter at a time. My suggestion is to read a chapter and immediately follow through with the given exercises, checklists, downloads, and templates. Give yourself time to implement them correctly and allow yourself to get into the habit of using them before moving on to the next chapter and thus the next step in the process.

Disclaimer: If you are currently a licensed real estate agent and will commit to this program for 90 to 180 days and be accountable to the actions I will ask you to do, this program will *completely* transform your business and your life, but you have to do the work. You must have the desire and the belief that after reading these chapters, you *can* and *will* do the work. After coaching and training professionals for more than eleven years, I've come to understand that I can't want it more than you do. I have put these chapters in a specific order for good reason, and you will want to complete each chapter before moving on to the next.

It's time to let go of all that you thought was true: your excuses and limiting beliefs, and your baggage, mind tricks, and bad experiences that have held you back from success. That's exactly why you purchased this book. You feel the need to break out of the rut you're in, but you don't know how. I ask you to give yourself a fighting chance. Build your business the right way. Listen, be open-minded, and do things differently.

For me it was extremely painful to acknowledge that it was time to pick up the broken parts of my life and reconstruct my thoughts, habits, and daily disciplines so that I could have everything my family and I deserve. It was extremely important for me to support my family, to have choices in the way I work and live, and to not be tied to a desk. In sales, there can be a lot of pain around rejection, and for women even more so. Rejection is a core fear of the female psyche. I'm not too proud to admit the countless nights I broke down and cried after exhausting days with nothing to show for my efforts. Picking myself up off the floor to do it again the next day was a miserable, humbling experience, but something happened . . . something changed . . . and I can't wait to share it with you.

Let's dive in!

Chapter 1:

FROM HOMELESS
TO HALF A MILLION

*There's no mystery about what needs to be done to make
the money and live the lifestyle you want except the mystery
of why you won't do it.*
—Karen Coffey

It was 10:00 a.m. on a warm Tuesday morning in June. I was sitting at my 1950s-style wooden desk in an office I shared with three other agents at a large real estate boutique firm in the Atlanta, Georgia area. For six months, I had attended trainings, been on agent caravans, tackled the mounds of paperwork required for every transaction, and learned the state and local laws and restrictions concerning real estate. Six months, every day, and

I hadn't sold one home—not one buyer, not one seller, nothing. Zero, zip, nada!

This day could have been like all the others, but it wasn't. It turned out to be the major turning point in my sales career and in my real estate philosophy. I just didn't know it yet.

One year prior to this, I had sold a small business to my business partners so that I could pursue my dream and my addiction of a career in real estate. Any salesperson worth their weight in salt will tell you how the adrenaline pumps through your veins in this business. For some it starts from a young age; mine was at age ten drawing house plans with a stick in the dirt-lined swamps of Central Florida. It beat running from the mosquitoes and alligators.

In 1995, I passed the grueling exams for real estate sales and got my license. I had been a stockbroker earlier in my career, and had passed the coveted Series 7 exams, so how hard could the real estate exam be?

Pretty hard, I discovered, but I passed and fully expected to be raking in the money fairly quickly. After all, my friends and family told me I would be perfect as an agent—perfectly ineffective, as it turned out. I'm not sure if any of you have ever experienced that kind of production—the zero kind. It will destroy you or motivate you.

My husband was fully supportive of my new role, and my son, who was twelve weeks old at the time, was being taken care of by a Swedish au pair we hired, whom he loved. My husband's job afforded us a very nice lifestyle. I obviously didn't need to make too much money.

Big house, two fancy cars, decorator on call—yes, the decorator had a key and would just leave stuff in my house. If I liked it, I paid for it and it stayed. If I didn't, she came by in a month or so to pick it up. We were living the suburban American dream with a newborn and not too many cares in the world until that Tuesday morning in June when I heard my name over the intercom system: "Karen Coffey, pick up line two. Karen Coffey, pick up on line two." That always made me feel extremely important in the beginning of my career because I knew I didn't have any clients, and the only reason the call was directed to me was because I was the agent on duty that day, and no one else was available.

It was my husband on the phone. He got to the point, short and sweet.

"I've been laid off. The company projections aren't as they anticipated, and my role has been eliminated. I'm packing my things and leaving the office."

I sat there stunned, not sure what the implications were. Head in hands and tears welling up, I knew better than to ask, "What are we going to do?" I had to figure out a way for us to stay afloat and do it fast or we would lose everything. The truth was that our world was built on sand and over $100,000 in credit card debt, coupled with an immature belief that the money would never run out. The future was incredibly bright…until it wasn't.

I hung up and took a moment to pray. *How will we make it, Lord? Please show me the way.* Five minutes, ten minutes, fifteen minutes went by when finally, in a flash of what seemed like divine inspiration, the solution hit me.

Even though I hadn't sold one house and had made zero dollars in sales at that point, I had been paying attention in those training classes, and I knew there were some downright horrible things I *did not* want to do. I had avoided all the salesy and embarrassing things so many agents do out of desperation because I didn't need the money that badly. The pain of embarrassment was far worse than the pain of not having any money.

My life was chill. I was under no pressure to sell. There was nothing pushing on me with enough force to make me do the things I didn't want to do. But a moment of truth had come in that phone call from my husband, and I had to make a choice. Would I keep trying to do real estate my way, or would the pain of losing everything be enough to push me to the point of doing things differently?

There's nothing like a little pain to create a freshly opened mind.

What was keeping me stuck, fearful, and broke? In that flash of inspiration, I understood three things:

1. I needed a Big Enough Reason to do the things that were uncomfortable for me but would rocket me to success.
2. My natural talents and abilities would not bring me the amount of business that I needed.
3. I needed something or someone to keep me on track.

My Big Enough Reason had just happened, and I was willing to do anything and everything to get a sale, a listing, a rental—anything! Now I just needed to figure out how to stay on track of it all. I also needed to use my natural talents and gifts in my business, and improve them.

But how does one do that?

I made it a personal mission to dig deep into research. I studied all the avenues of self-discovery that I could find in books, online, and by attending courses and programs so that I could solidly overcome my weaknesses and use my natural talents and gifts to sell more and earn more.

After years of research, I discovered an amazing free resource that allowed me to focus on what I was naturally good at so that

I could use my strengths, not my weaknesses, to increase my confidence, skills, and income. This resource was called the DISC Strengths Assessment Test, a quick five-minute assessment I found on the Tony Robbins website.

Those results forever changed the way I thought about my unique talents and abilities. I was able to see what really held me back from achieving success. From that point on, I did everything differently in my real estate business. I communicated more powerfully, and I better understood how to handle other people in a way that was important to them.

My DISC assessment told me I was a High D/High I. I will get into the specifics of what that means in a later chapter, but the following is a summary:

- I'm not good at details, so I should not do detail-oriented tasks.
- I have the attention span of a gnat, so I need to stay focused and present with each client.
- I am never content with the way things are. I constantly strive for the next level.
- I have a natural warmth that others respond to positively.
- I tend to talk too much, so I need to be more of an active listener.
- In my email communications, I sometimes come across as abrupt and rude because I get straight to the point. I need to remind myself to include salutations and pleasantries.

Now that I was aware of my strengths, I needed to create daily accountability in my business, but first I needed to determine what that would look like. Having some available credit on one of my cards and taking a *huge* leap of faith, I took $1,500 out and—here is the gem, the thing that every right-minded person with zero money does—I hired a part-time assistant for fifteen weeks to sit at my desk to do busywork so that I wouldn't. I created an environment of *no excuses* for myself. I knew that if she was sitting there 3.33 hours three days a week, I couldn't also be in that chair. If she worked ten hours a week at ten dollars per hour, I knew I could afford to keep her for fifteen weeks. If I hadn't made any money by then, I would have to let her go. To take it even further, I knew that when I came in to work every day, I was not going to sit and stare at her. No! I was going to do all those wonderful things I said I hated, but I was going to do them a little differently so I didn't feel embarrassed about being a real estate agent.

One ad in Craigslist and three applicants later, I found a wonderful lady who needed part-time work ten hours a week.

Debbie showed up on Monday for her first day on the job, and I had no idea what I was going to have her do because I had no sales, no listings, no buyers, and nothing in my pipeline. I decided that studying the MLS and marketing manuals would be a great place to start, and that's all I could think of.

I left her alone to get acclimated while I locked myself in the agency conference room to make some dreaded phone calls. I had heard that calling For Sale by Owner (FSBO) listings was a good way to get immediate business, so I made my first call.

Call #1:
Ring Ring
"Hello?"
"Hi, this is Karen Coffey with Northside Realty, and I was calling to see how I could help you sell your home."
"What? F*** you!"
He hung up.

Yep! True story. I promptly broke down crying and said I would never be able to do this. What had I done? My husband and I had no money, and like an idiot, I had put myself $1500 deeper in debt and hired someone to help me do nothing!

I got up, walked around the office, grabbed two donuts from the kitchen that a lender had dropped off, cried some more then quit for the day. I told my new assistant to continue studying the MLS documents until the end of her shift, and I would see her Wednesday.

The next day was our company sales meeting and agent caravan immediately after, so I didn't have time to do any calls that day, right? That was my excuse anyway. An agent caravan is when all the agents in the office carpool and preview homes that have just come on the market for sale. The purpose is to give constructive feedback to the listing agent so that they can best advise their sellers on price, condition, upgrades, and other aspects of the property. You usually see five to eight homes during the agent caravan, and that can take most of the afternoon. Relieved of my guilt for not making phone calls that day, I committed to try it again Wednesday when Debbie would be back in the office doing nothing. Great motivator!

When Wednesday came, I dug out an old-fashioned script that I'd gotten from my office. Every agent in town used this script, so I thought I should too. Some of it works, and some doesn't. I've spent years refining it, but this is what transpired.

Call #2:
Ring Ring
FSBO: "Hello?"
ME: "Um yes...uh, I was calling about your home for sale... um, are you the owner?"

FSBO: "Yes, that's me. How can I help you?"

ME: "Uh, yes, this is Karen Coffey with Northside Realty, and...um...I was calling to see how I could help you sell your home."

FSBO: "You can't! Well, unless you bring me a buyer."

ME: "Great! So, if I bring you a buyer, you're happy to pay the commission?"

FSBO: "Yes, but you're the tenth agent that's called today!"

ME: (*Oh, crap!*) "Well, at least ten of us are working!" (He laughed.) "So that's great you're paying the commission. Where are you guys moving to?"

FSBO: "Detroit. We have family there."

ME: "Nice! And when did you want to be there by?"

FSBO: "By the time school starts. Our daughter is seven."

ME: "Okay...I know you want to save the commission and sell it yourself, and I don't blame you, but I'm curious—how long do you think you'll try selling it yourself before you consider using an agent?"

FSBO: "We'll probably try to sell it for three weeks or so. We've sold our other two houses ourselves, so I think we'll be okay."

ME: "Awesome, so three weeks. What if there was a way I could net you the amount of money you need to move to Detroit and sell your home in the next thirty to sixty days? Would you be interested?"

FSBO: "Yes, but how?"

ME: "Well, let me do this. I'm going to send you a packet of information on how I get homes sold, not just listed. Take a minute to look at it, and I'll stop by on Saturday to go over how I can net you that money. Would ten in the morning be okay?"

FSBO: "Yes, that would be fine."

ME: "Will everyone who's on the warranty deed be there on Saturday? It's helpful if everyone sees the values and makes joint decisions."

FSBO: "Absolutely, we'll be here. We look forward to the package."

ME: "Great. See you Saturday!"

I immediately did the happy dance all over the conference room, jumping up and down, punching the air with my fists, resisting every urge to open the door and run laps around the office. I had a choice to make right then and there. Do I stay and continue calling my list of FSBOs, or do I quit while I'm ahead? It was a hard decision to make. In my thoughts, I kept hearing, "Should I stay or should I go, now?" from the song of the same name by The Clash.

I desperately wanted to go back to my office and tell Debbie what I'd just accomplished, but I couldn't. Why? When I hired her, I told her I was a busy agent who worked hard to get appointments every day, and here I was doing a happy dance around the office after making one appointment. I couldn't burst her bubble and let her find out that she was working for a clueless agent who had never sold a house!

Then I thought, *I could call my husband and tell him.*

But my next thought was *No!* I would stay the course and continue making calls until I went through all the phone numbers on the list, about ten. I didn't make any more appointments that day, but I did speak to a few people who said they would use an agent at some point. They weren't ready to list yet, so I told them I would send them some information and check back with them later.

Debbie and I were in business! She prepared four pre-listing packets and one Comparative Market Analysis (CMA) for me to take along with the listing paperwork I needed for Saturday.

In the next three weeks, I secured six new listings, sold two in the first thirty days, and got a qualified buyer under contract. Debbie was doing great! She was marketing the listings, taking care of the paperwork and files, and we were making money. In fact, we made so much money that my husband decided not to look for another job. Instead, he decided to get his real estate license and join me in the business.

It took a little under one year to replace his salary, but we did it. Disaster averted! We did, however, make some smarter choices by scaling down our living expenses. We moved into a smaller home and traded our cars for less expensive ones. The au pair had to go back to Sweden, and the decorator had to give her key back, but it was all for the best. There was peace of mind and a feeling of achieving a goal through adversity. My Big Enough Reason was definitely big enough to propel me and motivate me to succeed at things I had previously failed at miserably.

My newfound self-awareness and accountability put me at the top of my game in real estate, and my business showed no signs of slowing down. Because we harnessed successful skills and systems, our sales team was growing, and we were beating our sales records month after month.

Fast forward to 2008. I had now been a top-producing sales agent for over eleven years, consistently hitting number one in listings and sales year after year. I was also a regional sales trainer and coach. If you recall, something else happened in 2008—the real estate market crashed. Foreclosures and short sales accounted for approximately one out of every fifty-four homes in the country, the job market fell apart, and friends and family were losing their jobs in droves. Unemployment was at an all-time high.

I'd like to say I sailed through it unscathed, but I didn't.

My steady stream of real estate clients dried up, my coaching clients went away, and so did my income. I lost my house, my car, and my mother all in the same year, and along with a divorce, I lost all pride and self-respect. The next two years were hell, and I was literally drowning in poverty as a single woman with a small child.

Living in a friend's basement, deciding which flavor of Ramen noodles we would eat that day (no joke), I had nothing but time on my hands. I began studying mindset, personal development as well as other sales and business techniques and became a master at following and implementing models that other successful leaders had developed in their industries.

I began to understand how sales professionals could make a tremendous amount of money using their gifts, talents and mindset shifts. Now I needed skills and techniques that would work in any economic climate, the good, the bad, and the ugly. I vowed I would never let it happen again, the loss of everything. I had followed some well-known gurus over the years, but their systems seemed outdated and in need of an upgrade. I was living proof that in a down market, some of the things they taught just didn't work.

So I tweaked the systems and once again set out to master them. My gut told me the old-fashioned models and teachings weren't going to work for me and my style, so I rejected anything that seemed stuffy, salesy, outdated, and old-fashioned.

The market had shifted, and I was ready to do the same.

I moved to a new market and closed a consistent fifteen to twenty transactions each month and brought in a little over $100,000 in my first 100 days of being there, and that was from zero. I was on track to closing half a million that first year. Others began asking me how I did it and if I would help them. I documented everything and found that the results could be duplicated, but only if they combined the three strategies I mentioned earlier:

- Mindset
- Skills
- Systems

I didn't quite believe it when my world crashed around me, but it didn't take long to climb up from the bottom and achieve a level of success I had never known before. Even now, I see the results of this method every day for myself and for my clients, and it unleashed in me a passion for helping women be successful. My company and I now teach this method to agents, brokers, and real estate teams across the country so they can stop running businesses of overwhelm, boredom, and mediocrity, and instead bring excitement and success into their lives while earning an amazing and consistently high income while only working twenty to thirty hours a week. It's crazy, but it's true.

And it all begins with mindset, or what I call the Money Miracles and Breakthroughs Process.

Strategy #1: Mindset

Chapter 2:

THE MONEY MIRACLES AND BREAKTHROUGHS PROCESS

True abundance isn't based on our net worth;
it is based on our self-worth.
—Gabby Bernstein

call my mindset method the Money Miracles and Breakthroughs Process, because I see miracles happen every single day. This method uses motivation, visualization, gratitude, and a host of other wonderful practices that take just fifteen minutes every morning to implement. If you follow this process, you will completely transform your life in just a few short months.

So how did I discover this miraculous method and reap quantifiable benefits and results?

Some years ago, something bizarre happened to me that I rarely talk about due to the odd nature of it, but it changed my life and my business dramatically. I want to share it with you so that you can have the same great results I've had without going through the kind of traumatic, life-changing experience it took for me to harness this wisdom.

I had been working in real estate for many years, and my weeks consisted of running around like crazy with a semblance of a plan, but mainly just a lot of hours that made me feel busy. I was putting in fifty to sixty hours a week and was extremely stressed, running from sunup to sundown negotiating with not-so-friendly agents, and I was quickly losing my love for the business.

One Sunday afternoon, I wasn't feeling right. I was having chest pains, couldn't get up a flight of stairs without losing my breath, and felt tingling in my left arm and jaw. Convinced that I was having a heart attack, I went to the hospital, but the doctors assured me they could find no signs of heart failure, so they sent me home to rest. I was on bed rest for five days, and during that time, I was getting weaker and more despondent, and was so scared of what might be happening to me that I asked a friend to come over and pray with me. After heartfelt and fervent prayers, my friend left, and I felt no change. Still feeling weak, I went to bed.

The next day was extraordinary. Not the beginning of the day when I woke up already feeling exhausted before my feet hit the floor, but halfway through the day when I fell on my knees and asked a God I wasn't even sure I believed in to heal me and take the pain away. Not a religious person, I felt guilty even asking, like I only had so many requests in a lifetime, and I had used up all of mine.

I never could've imagined what happened next. I heard a voice say, "Go write."

Shocked out of my mind, I tried to push the voice out of my head, but it came again, twice more.

"Go write."

The only thing I could think of was that I had gone absolutely crazy. I would be put in a padded cell and never see my friends or family again. What the heck was going on?

When I heard this voice a third time, much stronger than the previous two times, I decided I might want to do what I was being told. I pulled out an old notebook I kept on my nightstand, opened it, and began writing the most beautiful words I had ever heard. No rhyme, no reason, just words on a page that somehow created a flow of sentences that made sense.

I wrote for about an hour, then put my pen down and realized there was no more pain, no more weakness, no more exhaustion. Whatever had me in its grasp was gone.

This continued every day for the next nine months. I took out pen and paper and wrote guided words of inspiration, wisdom, and encouragement for myself, my family, and my friends. This changed everything about my life and my perspective. I felt lighter, happier, safer, and more aligned with all the things I wanted in life. Some mornings, I intuitively wrote down my goals and dreams, and then sat in silence and waited; invariably, as if from nowhere, a subtle thought or idea would come to me as to how to achieve them.

I was fascinated! What had I tapped into? Was this my own intuition? Was this God speaking to me? What was it? I'll share more about this story later. Whatever it was certainly had some clout in making things happen in my life.

So, here's what I did. I began experimenting with how others could tap into this experience through a process of prayer, meditation, relaxing, and writing. I became very clear on what

I wanted to accomplish for the day, the week, the month, the year. I allowed myself to be completely quiet and still, closed my eyes, and visualized a successful outcome in each of those areas. I wasn't just seeing success in my mind. I was *feeling* success. I was experiencing what it felt like when my goals were attained. Sometimes the feeling brought an extreme, happy smile to my face; other times I laughed, and still other times it felt more like being content, happy, and fulfilled. I felt as though I was in complete partnership with something much greater than me, and I didn't have to make it happen. God was handling all the details. I just had to be clear on communicating what I wanted.

Through my travels the next summer, I met an author named Asara Lovejoy at a tradeshow in Denver. She had written a book called *The One Command*. I wasn't the least bit interested in her book, but she gave me a free copy. When I got home, I thought I might as well crack it open and see what her book was about.

She spoke of miraculous events that had happened in her life. Her story of loss was somewhat similar to mine, so my ears perked up. She had discovered a process to manifest the things she wanted in her life, and it started with what she called the One Command. The entire process is explained in her book, and I strongly recommend you read it to fully understand the power of it, but one step was to repeat the following sentence based on what you want in your life:

"I don't know how I _____. I just know that I do, and I am fulfilled."

The following is an example from her book:

"I don't know how I make $250,000 this year. I only know that I do, and I am fulfilled."

What Asara was saying in her book is that she was completely and utterly detached from *how* she accomplished her goal(s). If she desired something, she became very clear as to what it was. She visualized the successful attainment of it and repeated the phrase, "I don't know how I [lose twenty pounds, etc.]. I only know that I do, and I am fulfilled." The only change I made to her process was to add the words "Thank you, God," to the end.

The final piece of the Money Miracles and Breakthroughs Process came together for me in 2014: the mind-shifting power of gratitude.

We've been told since we were kids that we should be grateful, and of course I was, but not to the extent and to the level that I was about to take it.

A new agent had just started in my office and was having exceptional success. Not a day went by that he wasn't in the office at 8:30 a.m. finding new leads.

My office was about three doors down from his, and he usually kept his door open. One day, I could hear him on the phone calling some expired listings. He was looking to get appointments with them so he could list the homes, sell them for the client, and make a commission.

He was good at what he did and had a way of relaxing the homeowners, who often were disgruntled because their home hadn't sold yet. When the homeowners answered the phone, he leaned back in his chair and talked to them like they were old friends. One morning, he leaned a little too far back in his chair and flipped over backward onto the floor. What impressed the hell out of me is that he kept on talking! He never skipped a beat and closed the homeowner for an appointment.

Once I stopped laughing and made sure he was okay, I asked him, "What gives you such a positive outlook and so many great outcomes in your business even though you're a new agent?"

His two-word answer was, "The Magic."

"The Magic?"

"Yeah, the Magic is a philosophy of using gratitude to change your life. I learned about it in a book of the same name by Rhonda Byrne." He shuffled through his desk drawer. "Here, you can have this copy. It will change your life."

Just as I did with *The One Command*, I devoured *The Magic* and implemented it into my daily Money Miracles and Breakthroughs Process.

Within thirty days, I signed a coaching deal for $100,000 for the upcoming year!

Within the following thirty days after that, I signed a multiple six-figure coaching deal, and I was feeling happier. My mindset was extremely positive, and I realized that the right people were showing up in my life at the exact right time to make my goals and visualizations come to fruition.

It wasn't until seventy-five days into this new daily routine that something shifted in such a way that I knew there could be no coincidence, no other explanation. It wasn't a small something, but a whopping $595,000 in my bank account.

That would be the first of so many money miracles in my life that I could write a book on that topic alone. From that point on, every goal that I took through this process became a reality.

If you really want to incorporate the power of the Money Miracles and Breakthroughs Process, add these books to your library:

The One Command by Asara Lovejoy

The Magic by Rhonda Byrne (author of *The Secret*)

In this chapter, I will share with you every step of the Money Miracles and Breakthroughs (MMB) Process that led to my initial success, which continues to this day. Print it out, laminate it, and put it on your office wall or refrigerator door. Let it be a part of your success every day.

 The MMB Process of creating the success you want in your business consists of seven steps:

Step 1: Quiet your mind through prayer and meditation.
Step 2: Commit to accomplishing your objectives.
Step 3: Motivate yourself.
Step 4: Express gratitude.
Step 5: Detach from the how.
Step 6: Visualize the one thing you must do today.
Step 7: Journal your daily progress.

Step 1: Quiet Your Mind through Prayer and Meditation

Silence is an imperative part of the Money Miracles and Breakthroughs Process. It allows you to let go of the busyness of the day and start with a clean slate from which you can create your life and mold your business while asking for help from a power greater than you. For me that's God. For some it's the Universe that provides help in all things. The key is this: asking for help allows you to take your mind off the things that drain your energy and control you, and allows you to be spirit led.

Here's an example of a way to create silence through prayer and meditation.

Take a moment to breathe deeply and relax every muscle in your body. Start at your feet and imagine each group of large muscles in your body relaxing; move up through your calves, knees, and thighs, and then relax your stomach and your back muscles. You may want to play some soothing music to help you relax. Some find it helpful to imagine a feeling of warmth coming up through the bottom of their feet, like a warm light. Now, allow this warmth to come up into your shoulders; then, lift your shoulders up and drop them down. Imagine the warmth going down your arms into your wrists and hands. Now go back up to your shoulders and feel your neck muscles relaxing, then your scalp and your forehead; then, relax the muscles around your eyes, and lastly, relax your jaw.

Now, just be still and breathe for a few moments...let go of all that you think you need to do, and remember, the world revolves around the sun just fine without your help, so it's okay to let go.

This part of the process is very personal and depends on what you believe and how open-minded you are. I always say, "Holy Spirit, flow through me. All that I think I know I release to you. I am open to your guidance, your love, and your joy." After I speak these words, I usually feel a physical calmness in my body, and I know that I am connected with Spirit in that moment. By reaching out in prayer, I'm asking for help in creating success in my personal life, in my business, and in my finances—specifically, the success that is best for me. I also ask that the guidance bless all those around me.

Step 2: Commit to Accomplishing Your Objectives

I prefer not to use the word *goal* because goals have somehow migrated into wishes that never come true and New Year's resolutions that are never kept. We set them, life happens, and we never reach them. Even when we say the words, "My goal is to lose ten pounds, or my goal is to set four listing appointments this week," it feels like we're also saying, "Yeah, but don't hold me to it—it probably won't happen."

So I use the words "I am committed."

"I am committed to losing ten pounds."

"I am committed to setting four listing appointments this week."

Can you feel the difference in commitment statements versus goal statements?

"I am committed" says, "No matter what, no matter where, I will give it my all to ensure I achieve this."

So, each day in step 2, ask yourself what you are committed to in relation to your visualization.

Step 3: Motivate Yourself

Not all of us are motivated by money, trips, and acquiring the finer things in life. We are all different; what makes one person tick doesn't necessarily make another person tick.

Anthony Robbins, the author of *Unleash the Power Within*, talks about how we are motivated by pain or pleasure. We're either running away from pain or running toward pleasure. My initial success in real estate was due to running away from pain. There was nothing pleasurable enough to make me do the uncomfortable things I needed to do to succeed, but there was certainly enough pain. I would've done anything to avoid the pain of bankruptcy and foreclosure. Some of you know exactly what I'm talking about.

How does a person know what motivates them? Why is that important?

Answer these questions:

How would financially *succeeding* in my business affect me and/or my family this year? Be specific.

How would financially *failing* in my business affect me and/or my family this year? Be specific.

When you think about your answers to these two questions, which has the most emotional charge for you? You will either feel ecstatic about the rewards you and/or your family enjoy when you are successful, or you will feel extreme dread, fear, and anxiety from the pain of failing yourself and/or your family. That will tell you whether you are motivated by avoiding pain or pursuing pleasure.

When we are motivated by pleasure, we can post dream boards around our office with pictures of yachts, vacation homes, new cars, family photos, things that bring us pleasure and motivate us to do the hard things in sales like generate leads and prospect for new business on the phone. When I first learned this method, I noticed that I could surround myself with all kinds of positive outcomes and nice things, but nothing motivated me to get into action. You see, I was comfortable the way things were, maybe even complacent. I wasn't motivated by pleasure.

It wasn't until I saw the pain that could happen in my own life, if I didn't get busy selling, that I actually started making money.

When we are motivated by pain, it can sometimes be helpful to remind ourselves of the painful outcomes that can happen if we don't do the hard things. I never wanted to focus only on the negative, so I created two boards: one was my dream board, and the other was my impending disaster board. For me, it was imperative to focus on both, not just one or the other.

My pleasure board consisted of images and words that reminded me of what I was working toward: a healthy body, a huge savings and investment portfolio, a second home in the mountains, a picture of a happily married couple.

My pain board included pictures, words, and photos that represented everything I wanted to stay away from, things that reminded me that if I didn't do the hard stuff and muscle through the pain of rejection a couple of times a day, those pictures would become my reality. I had images of a house in foreclosure, the word REPO, overdraft charges, a couple arguing, and a woman in a hospital bed with her family standing around looking worried. Yikes! Powerful imagery of situations I never wanted to experience.

I placed my pain board to the left of my pleasure board as if it were in the past on a horizontal timeline. I even had a picture of me in the middle between the two boards, pain and pleasure. Call me crazy, but it worked!

It prompted me to think about which direction I wanted to go each day. Would I regress backward to all the pain of the past, or would I move forward to new horizons? It forced me to acknowledge that I couldn't stand still. I had to make a choice.

As part of your Money Miracles and Breakthroughs Process, create your pleasure and/or pain boards this week. Place them where you will see them every day.

Step 4: Express Gratitude

It's time we started being grateful for the things that our business is giving us, and stop complaining about what it's not.

The book *The Magic* instructs us to write ten things each day that we are grateful for, but each day they must be different. In other words, I couldn't put down that I was grateful for my health every day. I had to write a variation of that, such as "I am grateful for my eyesight today," or, "I am grateful that I can walk with ease."

As I expanded my gratitude during this twenty-eight-day program, I became aware of people, experiences, conversations, and business deals flowing to me out of nowhere. I began specifically writing ten things I was grateful for in my business every day. Instead of complaining about what business was *not* giving me, I became grateful for what it *was* giving me. Within thirty days, I had doubled my income, deals were flying in the door, referrals were coming my way, and lucky breaks were the norm. I was meeting people who turned out to be game-changers in my life, and all from applying the seven steps in this chapter.

Adding gratitude to this process was my way of making sure I started every day with a positive mindset. No matter what was going on in my life, good or bad, there was something to be happy about.

It isn't always easy to do this, but it's worth it.

Step 5: Detach from the How

To detach means to let go of any preconceived notion of how your commitments will pan out, and to let go of having your outcome happen in a certain way. Yes, I want you to have a vision, I want you to be grateful when it comes to fruition, but salespeople are notorious for being control freaks. We tend to have a mentality of "if it's to be, it's up to me." But that's not entirely true, is it? You are not solely responsible for making things happen in your life. Your heart beats fine without your help, and the earth revolves around the sun just fine without your help, so it's good to remember that there might be something else at play here besides your strong will. We can have a goal, we can have a commitment, and we will be proactive in achieving those goals, but let's make sure it is spirit-led action. Let's release the compulsion to know every step along the way, and trust that everything will fall into place if we're doing our part. It will come, I promise.

So, visualize what you want to create, ask for help, and detach from the how. This is where the One Command comes into play:

"I don't know how I_____. I only know that I do, and I am fulfilled!"

Let's fill in the blanks. Go back to the visualization and commitments you want to achieve this year, this month, or this week.

Examples:

I don't know how I make two listing appointments this week. I only know that I do, and I am fulfilled!

I don't know how I get two qualified buyers this week. I only know that I do, and I am fulfilled!

I don't know how I lose five pounds this week. I only know that I do, and I am fulfilled! Thank you, God!

I don't know how I save $1,000 for the holidays. I only know that I do, and I am fulfilled! Thank you, God!

It is crazy cool how this works! Just by repeating those words, you are letting go of the how. You are detaching from how the thing you desire gets done. When you do that, your mind automatically and almost instantaneously gives you an idea or suggestion for how to do it successfully.

Using the One Command samples above, write down some things you would like to create in your life or business.

I don't know how I _____. I only know that I do, and I am fulfilled!

Once you find one or two One Commands that you like, close your eyes and repeat them to yourself three or four times until the words resonate in your being. Again, don't be attached to how it will happen. Just keep saying, "I know that it does, and I am fulfilled."

Step 6: Visualize the One Thing You Must Do Today

Let's recap what we have learned so far:

You're still, quiet, and relaxed.

You've had some prayer and meditation time and allowed yourself to feel the results of your success.

You've made a commitment to yourself.

You've reminded yourself of what motivates you through pain and pleasure.

You've identified ten things you are grateful for.

You've practiced detaching from *how* something happens through the One Command.

Now you're ready for Step 6: Visualize the one thing you absolutely must do today to move you closer to your commitments.

You might be wondering, *Karen, I'm not sure how to practice visualization. What do I actually do while visualizing the one thing? Can you help me?*

Yes, I can, and I'm glad you asked! Let's take a moment to talk about visualization.

Visualization is about using the power of your mind and imagination to manifest the successful attainment of your goals in specific detail. It allows you to experience your goals fully before they happen.

As the late Wayne Dyer wrote in his book *Wishes Fulfilled: Mastering the Art of Manifesting,* "By believing passionately in something that does not yet exist, we create it. The nonexistent is whatever we have not sufficiently desired."

Notice a key word in what he wrote.

Passionately!

By believing passionately in something that does not exist, we create it. He didn't say believe passively or to be semi-excited about it, but believe *passionately* in anything, and you can create it.

At this step of visualization, I allow thoughts and ideas to come and go until something excites me. In other words, I am excited that the visualization I am imagining is the right one for me to focus on that day or week. You may have a visualization that you want to focus on for a week, or you may want to focus on a different one every day. Follow your gut instinct with this. I think you'll know which is the best decision for you. I've had some clients visualize the successful outcome of the same thing every day for a month.

Visualization is using your imagination to create a successful event, scenario, or experience in your mind's eye so that you can focus on it and be open to ideas on how to create it.

Take a moment to breathe and relax. Ask God to help you.

Imagine that today is the last day of the year, and you're discussing the success you've achieved this year with your friends and family members. They are extremely happy and excited for you, and they ask you to describe how you achieved such great success. As you share the incredible results with them, notice how you feel. Notice if there is a smile on your face or a sense of excitement inside you.

Now imagine other things that you accomplished this year, such as a surplus in your bank accounts, college tuition paid with ease, bills paid on time. Notice your sense of calm. Everything has been so easy for you and almost effortless this year. Imagine some of the rewards you earned or were able to give to yourself and others. How did that make you feel?

Can you smell the leather of a new car or the salty air of the ocean as you dig your toes in the sand on your island beach vacation?

Now imagine the happy clients that you were able to help this year. Take a moment to really feel the satisfaction that resulted from the service you provided these people and their families just by doing what you do best. You helped them find a home and all the blessings that come with that. You were the answer to their prayer, and you are so happy that you put yourself out there so you could help them.

Now, take yourself in your imagination to the end of your current month. It's the last day of the month, and you're looking back at a very successful sales month. What would that look like in terms of dollars earned? How would that make you feel? Now think about all the things you were able to do because of that successful month. Continue to breathe and relax...take your time to visualize these things. Your mind is a muscle that needs to be exercised, just like your body, so it can become stronger and more powerful.

Now imagine it's Friday night, and you are sitting down with your favorite beverage with a smile on your face and a feeling of *YES! What a fantastic week!* Take a moment to feel it. Don't worry about the "how" right now; just stay in the feeling of accomplishment, financial ease, and success, whatever success means to you. Imagine your business growing without any effort; it's just so easy for you. The conversations that you have are fun, your lead generation initiatives are bringing in tons of leads, you have time with your family and friends, you have several qualified appointments every week, and they are all signing purchase agreements. Feel the satisfaction of building a successful business.

Lastly, I want you to imagine an amazingly productive day today. If you want to have that awesome feeling at the end of the week, at the end of the month, and at the end of the year, what would you need to do today to make that happen?

Script how you want today to be. What results will you attain? Imagine leads, clients, and customers responding to you in a positive way. They want to talk to you because they need what you have, and they know you can deliver it. It would be selfish of you to keep all that from them, so you don't even try. Smile and enjoy the movie you are creating in your mind.

This is the art of visualization—to see, hear, feel, and believe passionately in your dreams so they become reality. Make them as real as possible in your imagination first, and the world and everything in it will conspire to make it your reality.

Now, let's apply this practice to visualizing the one thing you must do today to keep your business on track and make steady progress toward accomplishing your objectives.

Visualization helps you to see where you want to go; it helps you commit to your objectives and stay motivated and full of gratitude; it helps you to detach from the how. Now you are ready to ask yourself the following question:

What is the one thing I must do today that will ensure I make my commitments a reality?

You probably already know exactly what it is. When the answer comes to you, write it down in your notebook or journal. If you don't, you'll forget, and before you realize what has happened, you will have lost your way.

Visualizing the one thing you must do today, then repeating that practice every day, is how you will make steady progress toward meeting your objectives and accomplishing unimaginable success in your business.

As a resource, I've included a pre-recorded guided visualization on our private Making Agents Wealthy Resource page at karencoffey. com/resources. When you complete your visualization, take out a journal and immediately write down your vision, any feelings or thoughts, people you saw, and so on. Writing it down gives you a sense of purpose, and it serves as a great reminder of what you visualized.

Step 7: Journal Your Daily Progress

Purchase a notebook or journal that you will use only for the Money Miracles and Breakthroughs Process. You will want to keep it long after you have written down your divine inspirations so that you can go back and review. You will be absolutely amazed at what you wrote, and you may not have realized that the answers to the questions or statements you wrote came to you later, somehow inspired by something you saw in your visualization.

I always like to write the aha moments of what I see, how I feel, and the things I'm grateful for, not only so I have a record of them, but because I don't want to forget.

I am frequently asked, "What do you journal?"

My suggestion is to write down any thoughts, ideas, or directions that come to you during your visualization. Maybe while you were playing your mental movie you saw a scene you didn't expect, something that excited you or made you happy. Write it down. Write down anything you must do today to accomplish the successful week you visualized.

Another very powerful practice that can be part of this step is prayer. My prayer has always been, "Father, who can I help today? What do you want me to know today? Give me direction, and give me clarity."

You may not feel comfortable doing these practices, but after a few days of being persistent with this practice, you will realize that your mind is looking for answers to the visions you placed there. Your mind now understands that you mean business, and this isn't a fluke. You are creating your reality with or without it, and it needs to jump on board or it's going to get left behind.

It's easy and fun to do, it sets the right tone for your day first thing in the morning, and it exponentially changes your results that day and thereafter.

Provided below is a sample Weekly One Page for you to use as inspiration to create your own. Post it in your office to remind you that you can create your life and your business the way you want it, or you can allow others to scatter you and your day to the wind. It's your choice.

Weekly One Page

KAREN *Coffey's*
MAKING AGENTS
WEALTHY

My vision for this week is?

I am committed to:

Pain & Pleasure

My pleasurable motivators that I'm motivated to obtain? (savings, pride in self, independence, college, 2nd or 3rd home, yacht, consistent income, etc.):

My painful motivators that I'm motivated to avoid? (debt, a job, lack of independence, sleepless nights, etc.):

Gratitude: 10 things I am grateful to my business for today:

1)   4)   7)   10)
2)   5)   8)
3)   6)   9)

Detach:

"I don't know how I _____, I only know that I do...and I am fulfilled!!!

Inspiration:

What is the One Thing I need focus on today to make my commitments a reality?

www.KarenCoffey.com

Strategy #2: Skills

Chapter 3:

YOUR AUTHENTIC SELLING STYLE

Life is not about finding yourself; it's about CREATING yourself.
—Shanna Ferrigno

I n chapter 1, I mentioned the DISC Strengths Assessment Test. When I took this test, it opened up a whole new world of understanding about my personality traits and how they affect my business. I was able to discover my natural strengths and determine how they could help me achieve success. I believe the DISC test can be a powerful tool for helping you harness your strengths too. Let's learn more.

Each of us has styles, strengths, and characteristics that make us shine. We've often thought of them as curses as well as blessings, especially when we have certain strengths that seem natural to us yet others don't have them, and that's frustrating.

You're more than likely a seasoned human being. You know that you are different from your family members, coworkers, and friends. This is *great* news, and you will learn to use those differences to your advantage, but first you need to discover what your awesome life-changing strengths are.

 Take fifteen minutes right now to go to karencoffey.com/resources to complete the DISC Strengths Assessment Test. When we send you the results, usually within twenty-four hours, take a moment to read over your findings and underline your strengths. If you would like us to go over the results with you and guide you on how these strengths translate into greater real estate sales, we'll be happy to do that! Just go to www.karencoffey.com/book and set up a time for us to walk you through the results.

More than two million people around the world have taken this test to better understand their behavioral styles. As Tony Robbins has stated, "Research shows that the most successful people share the common trait of self-awareness. They recognize the situations that will make them successful, and this makes it easy for them to find ways of achieving objectives that fit their behavioral style."

Now that you've taken the DISC assessment, let's talk about how you will use the results to create a no-nonsense, fast-growing business based on your strengths. By knowing your strengths, talents, and natural gifts, you will be able to quantum leap your sales because people will be attracted to you instead of you having to chase them down, which is repelling. They won't even realize that they want more of what you have to offer, and you will have fun growing your career. You'll enjoy your work and enjoy the people you choose to work with.

I want you to shine so brightly in all that you do that people clamor to be around you!

I was giving a talk at a conference when a beautiful young lady came up to me afterward and said, "You are the most energetic, shiniest person I know, and I loved your presentation!"

Another came up and said, "You know, if you're not giving, you're not living, and I can tell you're living and giving in a grand way."

Why would they say those things? I surely wasn't aware of anything I had done to receive those kind remarks. As an awkward teenager and child, I certainly did not start out as an energetic, shining person who attracted people to me. I had red hair, which I thought was ugly and made me look different, and I was five feet eleven inches tall with buckteeth. It took me a while to discover and believe that I had *any* talents at all. What changed? Self-awareness. I decided I wanted to know who Karen *really* was, and eventually, I knew myself so well that I was comfortable in my own skin and actually began to like who I was.

You may be confident and very self-aware, or you may be awkward like I was. Regardless, I want to take you to the next level by highlighting your natural talents, and the DISC assessment will help you capitalize on those.

Let's take a closer look at your results. On page two of your results report that was emailed to you, you will see two graphs that look like the images below:

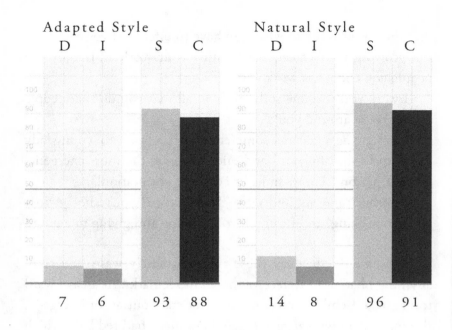

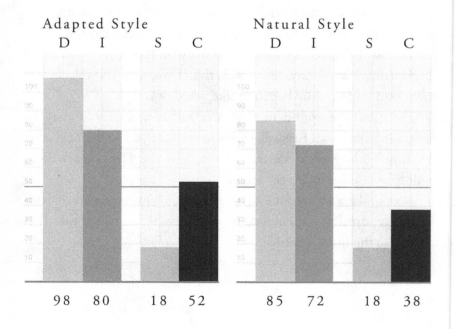

As you can see in the examples above, one graph shows your *adaptive style* score. This is how you act when you think others are watching you; you're adapting to please someone else. Usually, your adaptive style is prevalent within your work environment, or when you're under stress, or when you're not being your authentic self. You feel like you're being observed. When we stay too long in our adaptive style, we burn out because we are forcing ourselves into a behavioral pattern that is not natural to us.

The second graph shows your *natural style* scores. I love the natural style! This is your authentic self, who you are when you're relaxed and comfortable. Focus on your natural style score, because this is the real you. If you focus too much on adapting yourself to please others, you will be very unhappy, and you'll burn out in your sales role.

As we discussed earlier, your test results will be categorized by four letters: D, I, S, C. Let's take a closer look at what these represent.

For most people, two letter categories will score predominantly higher than the other two. For example, in the first graph shown above, the I and D are above the 50 percent line, so they are the predominant personality traits in that person's score.

You'll notice that in the second graph, the C and the S are above the 50 percent line, and the same is true with the I and S in the third graph. What does this mean for your real estate business? Let me give you an example from my life.

About five or six years ago, when I had moved more fully into a coaching role with agents, I had the honor of observing other coaches speak with real estate agents in my state. It was fascinating! They could zero in on that agent's challenges and come up with a plan in a matter of seconds. My jaw was on the floor. They immediately assessed each agent's strengths, and how those could benefit them in business. They also assessed each agent's challenges.

My lead coach at Karen Coffey Coaching puts it this way:

"When I took the DISC test, it felt like somebody had been following me around for a week! It was a crazy feeling but a good feeling, and more importantly, a validation. What I took away from the DISC experience is that you don't have to be like everybody else to be successful in this industry. You don't need to be boring and mediocre. The beauty of the real estate industry is that those who honor who they are authentically can layer the systems they love the most and focus on their individual style to achieve success.

Let's break the letters down into general descriptions and examine how you can use your strengths to your advantage as a successful real estate agent.

D

The D stands for *dominance*. The High D person can be described as driven, determined, direct, and to the point. Those with a prominent D are people who get things done. Show me someone who has been enormously successful in business, and I'll show you a High D. They are typically thinking four steps ahead of where they are, so they seem like they're not listening to you, but they are—and they're also thinking about what they need to do next. Most other types think High D people are rude because they don't engage in pleasantries, like asking how your weekend was, and to be honest, they don't really care. They're focused on their goals and objectives, and prefer to get straight to the issue or situation that needs attention. High Ds are competitive and want to win, but often they are only competitive with themselves.

At a party, the High D will tend to stand back and look around with a detached demeanor that says, "I'm here, and people will approach me if they want to talk to me."

High D Strengths in Real Estate

- Cold calling and door knocking
- FSBOs and Expired Listing strategies
- Working with affiliate partners and sponsors
- Building a team
- Dominating their market

High D Weaknesses in Real Estate

High Ds hate wasting time or being taken advantage of, and they can bulldoze over others at times. They have the tendency to be a bossy know-it-all because they really do (know it all), but they can come across as brash. Agents with a predominant D score need to learn to slow down and listen. If this describes you, realize that others do not work at the pace or level that you do. Consider this an opportunity to practice your leadership skills instead of allowing it to be a source of frustration.

Paperwork is a weakness for High Ds because they have no patience with what seems like busywork.

When a new client of ours came to the first call with one of my coaches, she brought her schedule for everyone on her team. She was a High D, off the charts. We immediately noticed that she had everyone working seven days a week. When asked why, she said, "Well, I work seven days a week, so why shouldn't they?" That is a High D. They tend to be workaholics and think everyone should be more like them.

Those with a High D score need to learn to slow down and show compassion and empathy.

I

The I stands for *influence*. This is because a High I person is always influencing someone. They can persuade almost anyone to do anything. Words such as inspiring, integrated, and inclusive describe them. They are the life of the party. Their mentality is, "Hey, I want to bring you along for the ride." When a High I person walks into the room, you know they're there. They are the shiny people! They have a glow. They often stand out with their verbal expressiveness, their body language, and their sense of style. When you talk about the person who is going to wind up with a lampshade on their head at the party, it's the person with a High I. They love flattery and are very optimistic about life in general.

High I Strengths in Real Estate
- Parties: housewarming parties, seller packing parties, client appreciation parties
- Open House events
- Tradeshows
- Networking

High I Weaknesses in Real Estate
High I people tend to go too fast and miss the details. They talk so much that they forget to listen. Conversations tend to be about them because they have much more interesting lives than most people have, mainly because they get bored easily. Also, they hate rejection, so they don't like to do anything they aren't excellent at. Do *not* ask them to play games like Monopoly because they hate losing.

The High I person needs to slow down and listen. Paperwork is a real weakness for this person because they don't pay attention to details.

S

Most people in the world are a High S. The S stands for *steadiness*. These are the people you can count on. They are consistent and often systematic in their approach. They're very stable in terms of temperament, emotions, what they do, and how they do it. Frankly, we need High S people to keep the wheels on the bus. Those with High S scores love family, comfort foods, and loyalty. Most of us love to have them in our lives because we know that we can count on them.

At a party, the High S tends to cluster with a loyal group of friends or family. More on the shy side, they won't go out of their way to meet new people but will be friendly to those who approach them.

High S Strengths in Real Estate
- Working with buyers, because of the ability to listen and understand their needs
- Follow-up; often do well with FSBOs
- Hosting parties and get-togethers such as Open Houses and outdoor barbeques
- Checklists! Tell them what to do and how to do it, and they will.
- When combined with a High C, excellent at handling the volumes of paperwork required of every real estate transaction
- If combined with a High I, perfect for working with buyers and not getting bogged down in paperwork

High S Weaknesses in Real Estate

1. High S people dislike change and are usually slow to make decisions. They also may get caught up in the transaction versus continuing to find new business.
2. And because they have a fear of the unknown and don't like to take risks, they sometimes miss opportunities.

Those with a High S score need encouragement to push themselves to do what's uncomfortable and to build their confidence by taking risks.

C

C stands for *conscientious*. The High C person strives for compliance, correctness, and being concise in everything they do. Accurate and detail oriented, High C people enjoy being very regimented in their approach. Their highest values are accuracy and perfection. Their mantra is, "I'll do it right no matter how long it takes." The work they do is judged by how they do it and the protocol they follow. An engineer, CPA, or architect might be a High C as well as military personnel or police officers. Those with a High C tend to be overly critical of others and how they do things. Perfectionism is their life. Their greatest fear is being criticized for doing something wrong. They tend to be risk averse.

The introverted High C is not typically at the party, and if they are, you'll find them in a quiet corner counting the minutes until they can go home.

High C Strengths in Real Estate

- Can be phenomenal brokers due to the compliance required of that role

- Accuracy with paperwork, numbers, and reviewing the transaction
- Online lead generation, due to the skill involved with details such as ad stats (clicks and views), search engine optimization, and Google search algorithms
- Social media, because they tend to be tech savvy

High C Weaknesses in Real Estate

1. High C people can get so bogged down in the details of transactions currently in progress that they forget to look for new business.
2. They can ask too many questions that aren't always important and can let that get in the way of moving forward.
3. Slow moving and methodical, High Cs can be too slow for most other types, whereas the High D is too fast.

Those with a High C score need to trust the process and move past the details to be successful.

Now that we have a basic overview of the personality styles, how does this information help us build a successful real estate business?

Wait a minute, you may be thinking. *There's only one chapter in the Skills section, and we've only talked about a personality assessment! Where is the list of skills I need to be successful?*

They're already inside you.

What *isn't* inside of you are the systems, which we will discuss next.

When I'm coaching agents on the importance of lead generation and how one size does not fit all, I tell them, "You can generate leads a thousand different ways. The trick is to find what you are naturally skilled at and enjoy doing." This is true for you too. When you discover what you love and are good at, stack those talents together, like layering a cake, and don't stop doing those things, no matter what. Combine those with systems and pretty soon you will have a process that works like a well-oiled machine.

If you are a new agent, chances are when you got your license you signed up with a brokerage. They welcomed you with a hug and a packet of paperwork to sign, and left you to your own devices to figure out how to make big money. Maybe they partnered you with a veteran agent, but you soon figured out that she's not skilled at lead generation either.

So you set off from one training class to another, only to discover you really, really hate phone work, and you would rather stick a needle in your eye than go door-to-door or to another networking event.

What do you do then?

Take a close look at your DISC test results and focus on your strengths. You don't have to be good at all things all the time, just a few things.

In the real estate business, you'll be surrounded by lots of different personalities among your fellow agents, service providers, and your clients. It is extremely helpful if you know how to communicate with them in a way that is comfortable for them and that allows you to close more of your transactions so that you can earn more money. That can be accomplished when you understand your personality strengths. When you become more familiar with the DISC assessment, you'll be able to deduce the strengths of others more easily too.

That's the beauty of the DISC assessment. By having a better understanding of your own style, you'll be able to recognize the styles of others. That will catapult your success in the industry. We often hear about the golden rule: "Do unto others as you would have them do unto you." I want you to throw that rule out the window. It's not about the golden rule. It's about the platinum rule. The platinum rule is, "Treat people the way they want to be treated."

Does a High D want a long, deep conversation and long emails? No! Bullet points only, please!

Does a High I take it personally when you don't talk to her at a party? Yes, because she's sensitive. Take the time to seek her out and talk to her.

Does a High S thrive when someone is barking commands? No. They prefer checklists and to-do lists.

Does a High C like you to talk in bullet points, or do they want the whole story? Whole story, please, with lots of details.

As you gain a deeper understanding of the strengths and weaknesses of your clients, friends, and family members, you will be a more responsive agent who is able to show empathy and compassion as you help your clients navigate the often-stressful process of buying a home. People will sense this and gravitate to you. You will learn to be a chameleon so your clients feel comfortable with you. This will give them such a great experience that they will tell others about you, and your business will grow.

In the next section, we'll get into the details of adding $100,000 to your business, but don't be tempted to set aside the techniques I've shared with you in this section. None of this works if you don't know your authentic self: how to maximize your strengths for effective sales and capitalize on those for a substantial income. The DISC assessment will help you do that.

We've seen how the right *mindset* and your unique *skills* can help you reach your highest potential, but a third element is vital for true success. You also need the right *system*. The biggest mistake most agents make is to fall back into old habits and patterns. I realize those can be hard to change, but what's the alternative? Another year of mediocre results? Not for you! Not this year!

I want you to reach your highest potential in all that you do. In the next section, we will explore Strategy #3: Systems. I will give you the exact steps you need to make $100,000 in 100 days, and to end the year with a multiple six-figure income—even if you are brand new to real estate sales or you've relocated to a new market and are starting over.

Strategy #3: Systems

Chapter 4:

YOUR MILLION-DOLLAR-DAY SCHEDULE

*Learning is not attained by chance; it must be sought for with
ardor and attended to with diligence.*

—Abigail Adams

Before we dive in to this section, I want to ask you a question. Have you ever gone to a class or seminar where you heard the most incredible information on a specific topic, and you said to yourself, "This stuff is amazing! I can't wait to implement everything I learned today! It's going to change my life!" Then, when it was over, you got in your car, and in the blink of an eye that funny thing called life happened?

Emails, texts, and voicemails jerk us back to what some call reality, but I don't believe that has to be our reality. I believe we can create the reality we want. It takes discipline, and not just a little; it takes a lot of discipline, in my experience. That's why the first step to creating the wealth and the life you want is the discipline of time management. That is achieved by having great systems in place.

A system is a set of connected components that form a complex whole. A system doesn't work well without its various parts, so I encourage you to remember that a system is intended to help you work better, faster, and with greater endurance. Here is how it all works together: The Money Miracles and Breakthroughs Process gives you the right mindset to set you up for success every day. Being aware of your authentic style, skills, and talents will keep you strong and confident as you work your natural strengths to your advantage. But, all the tools and techniques in this book will take you nowhere if you don't do them every day using a proven system to gain maximum results.

So let's go!

The alarm goes off, you hit snooze, and you roll over with a moan. Another day in paradise, huh? Even before your feet hit the floor, you feel overwhelmed and distraught with all the things you need to accomplish that day, and you have no idea where to begin.

Okay, you say to yourself, *one step at a time...take the dogs out, get the kids up and out of the house, take a shower and try to eat something semi-healthy and quick.* You check your emails and Facebook messages while you brush your teeth. (Come on, you know you do it!) It's only eight in the morning, and three agents are calling you with their hair on fire. One has a buyer whose loan approval went south, so they can't buy your listing; another agent can't get a lockbox open and wants you to drive out to the house to open it; the other is complaining because you forgot to have your buyer initial page ten of a forty-page contract, and by the way, the inspection came back with thirty-three items needing to be repaired. Do you feel me?

You call all of them back immediately to put out the fires, you drive to fix the lockbox, and then you spend the next three hours on the phone with lenders, inspectors, and several cranky agents who should have retired twenty years ago. Before you know it, your day has disappeared into the abyss. No new business has come in because all you've done is put out fires. Ugh!

My dad called this the tail wagging the dog.

It's a hard truth, but we all need to face it: most agents have *no* boundaries—personal, business, or otherwise.

We have been taught by well-meaning folks in the industry to be available 24/7 out of *fear* of missing a deal, *fear* of not having a closing, *fear* of not making money.

Well, that's not healthy!

And it's also crazy!

No other industry teaches its professionals to drop everything and run out of the house at all hours of the day and night to go meet some stranger who says they want to do business with you! Most real estate agents don't even ask if the buyer is pre-qualified. They just grab their keys and go.

Here's the truth: if you create boundaries in your business and in your personal life, and you treat your business more like a business than an on-call emergency service, you will have a consistent flow of leads, clients that respect your time, and most importantly, a consistent flow of income each month. How does that sound?

Let me be the first to tell you:

THERE ARE NO REAL ESTATE EMERGENCIES!

Really, there aren't. The world would like you to think that everything is an emergency and needs to be done right now. They know you can't get away from them because of texting, emails, social media messaging, and the hundreds of other apps that keep us connected 24/7.

My suggestion:

Stop the madness before it burns you out and creates an extreme financial burden on you or debilitates you with stress.

Three years into my real estate career, I was averaging $200,000 to $250,000 a year in net commissions. I was working fifty to sixty hours a week trying to keep up. I had my part-time assistant, and I hired someone to call expired listings for me to try to get listing appointments.

I was livin' the dream!

Combine that with my husband's income, and we had a 6,000-square-foot house on the lake, a second home in the mountains, three fancy cars, a private-school education for our son—and I was miserable. I had created a living hell for myself and didn't even realize it.

Our role as real estate agents is *not* to run around like crazy people hoping someone will use us to buy, sell, or invest in a home. It's not our role to get upset when our family members use another agent. Our role is to facilitate a smooth, enjoyable, and maybe even phenomenal real estate transaction while taking care of ourselves, our families, and our finances in an enjoyable way.

To accomplish this, we need to create a very predictable and consistent business that will give us everything we want and need. The key words here are *predictable* and *consistent*. You may know how it feels to have a few great months in a row, only to look at your business a few months later and see no closings on the horizon, not now or in the immediate future. I want to solve that for you.

Remember when I said there are no real estate emergencies? Don't put time in your schedule for handling them. Of course, you'll always need to communicate with people to get the transactions to the closing table, but you'll learn to do that at the appropriate times. You'll see what I mean on the next page.

Maybe you're thinking, *Why do I need to worry about time management and a schedule? I don't have any business yet!*

That's exactly why you need a system in place to help you with time management. When you don't have business, you're tempted to go to more training classes than you need and go on every agent caravan or Open House event because it makes you "feel" busy.

At this point, I want to introduce a term you may or may not be familiar with called money-generating activities (MGAs). Note: these are not lead-generating activities. These are money-generating activities. There is a big difference. Do you want leads, or do you want money? Exactly!

The following are the top five money-generating activities you will do as a real estate agent:
- Lead generation
- Lead follow-up
- Buyer and seller appointments
- Contract negotiations
- Fulfillment to current clients

Every day—whether you hand-write this, type it and print it out, or text it into your schedule—block off time for MGAs. Why? If you don't put it in your schedule, you won't do it.

Tony Robbins once said years ago, "Repetitious boredom is the mother of skill." If you are doing the same thing day in and day out, you will master it.

Do you want to be the master of your craft or a mediocre representation of it? You want to be a master!

The following elements ensure that you'll be a master at making money from residential real estate sales. These must be a part of your work schedule every day:

- Schedule your vacations and time off for the year. Do this before you schedule anything else. Discuss this with your spouse, family, or significant other, and decide where you'll go and when.

- Schedule some quiet time to follow the seven steps listed in chapter 2 where we learned about the Money Miracles and Breakthroughs Process.

- Schedule time to exercise—stretching, yoga, weights, walking, running, swimming—whatever works best for you.

- Schedule time to do your money-generating activities. Focus on these five: lead generation, lead follow-up, buyer and seller appointments, contract negotiations, and fulfillment to current clients.

- Schedule some daily downtime and fun!

Below is my Million-Dollar-Day Schedule. I call it that because for every week I worked this schedule, I could expect a million dollars in appointments, and appointments lead to closings and more money!

Your Million-Dollar-Day Schedule

7:00 a.m.–7:30 a.m.: Wake up, MMB Process

7:30 a.m.–8:30 a.m.: Exercise, breakfast

8:30 a.m.–8:45 a.m.: Get to the office, get prepared for money-generating activities, go over daily One Page

8:45 a.m.–10:30 a.m.: Money-generating activities

10:30 a.m.–11:00 a.m.: Lead follow-up, notes, packages, plan events, past client follow-up, Six-Figure Open House follow-up (see chapter 7)

11:00 a.m.–1:00 p.m.: Return phone calls, emails, Facebook, paperwork, negotiate contracts

1:00 p.m.–7:00 p.m.: Appointments

After 7:00 p.m.: Quality time with yourself, family, and friends

Do this Monday through Thursday every week, and you will never have to worry about whether you'll have consistent earnings. If you cannot currently work these hours starting at 8:30 a.m., adapt this schedule to a later start time.

 What Will Your Power Schedule Be?

Take a moment to put this in motion right now. Grab your calendar, planner, phone notes app, or whatever method works best for you. Write down the money-generating activities you will do for each day this week. Be as specific as you can. Schedule those activities into certain hours of the day. Each time you look at your schedule, you will feel a sense of urgency to get these MGAs done.

Here is a final tip on time management and scheduling:

People will treat you the way you tolerate being treated. I should say that again. People will treat you the way you tolerate being treated, and that goes for our clients, our leads, other agents, our friends, and even our family members.

I can't change whether your family respects you, but here are some tips on getting your clients and leads to respect your time:

Don't answer the phone every time it rings. Let it go to voicemail so they hear the following message and understand your boundaries.

"Hi, you've reached the cell phone voice mail of _____with XYZ Realty. My/Our hours are from _____ to _____ Monday through Friday and Saturdays by appointment. If you've reached this message after hours, we'll get back to you the next business day. Thanks for calling, and have a great day!"

A few things happen that I *love* when I use this voice message.

- It is clearly understood that I don't work Sundays.
- Buyers know they'll need an appointment if they want to see properties on Saturdays.
- Agents submitting contracts on one of my listings know that they will not hear from me after 7:00 p.m. This allows time for more offers to come in, and there is nothing wrong with that. Sometimes another offer is a better offer!
- If there is a real estate "emergency" after 7:00 p.m., chances are it will have been taken care of before 9:00 a.m. the next day. Thus, it was never an emergency in the first place. (Remember, there are no emergencies in real estate!)

Meet with your family to discuss your commitments to your business, why it's important to you, and how they can support you.

My work schedule was a chaotic mess when I worked fifty to sixty hours a week. The stress was incredibly hard to deal with, and then I had my scary experience when I thought I was having heart complications. After implementing what I wrote down that day in my bedroom, I began working only four days a week, Monday through Thursday, 9:00 to 7:00 p.m. I rarely had appointments on the weekends, and I was home by 7:00 p.m. each night. I only worked eight out of twelve months that year because I wanted to enjoy the holidays like I'd never been able to do, and get this: I made $2,000 more than I had the year before, simply by following what I had written down.

It changed my life, and from that point on, everything I did was with time management in mind. I scheduled everything.

There is a harsh and heartbreaking reality I've learned over the years, one that not many people talk about, and one I feel I must talk about in this section on schedules and boundaries. So many agents get into this industry and do what all the other agents are doing, which is chasing, running, and abandoning family and friends to make a deal happen. I am begging you—please, please, please don't do this to yourself or your marriage. It's all fun and games in the beginning, but then you wake up one day and everything is falling apart. Divorce rates are extremely high in the real estate industry. Stress and working long hours are taking their toll on our health and relationships. In October 2016, the *New York Times* reported that a global study showed that women are now drinking as much as men, and heart disease is on the rise. That is why it is imperative to do this business the right way and not the same old-fashioned ways that have been taught for more than a hundred years.

Your Million Dollar Day Schedule

Time	Agenda & Focus	Projects/Goals
7-8	Wake Up, Mindset, Motivation, Prayer & Meditation, Visualization, Journaling & Exercise	
8:30	Get to the office & Prepare for MGA's	
8:45-10.30	Money Generating Activities	
10:30 - 11:00	Lead Follow up, Notes, Packages, Texts	
11:00 - 1pm	Return calls, Emails, Facebook & Paperwork	
1-7pm	Appointments	
7pm & on	Quality time with yourself, friends & family	

Do this Monday through Thursday every week and you will never have to worry about where your consistent income is going to come from.

Repetitious boredom is the mother of skill.
~ Tony Robbins

Notes

Create your own powerful schedule using the Million-Dollar-Day Schedule as an example. Be sure to schedule time off, quality time, and of course, priority #1, your money-generating activities for a minimum of four days a week. Also Record your voicemail given to you on page 60.

In the next chapter, I will share the first money-generating activity (MGA) you must do, or you'll leave thousands of dollars on the table. When you write an MGA on your Million-Dollar-Day Schedule, make it the first thing you do that day. Get it out of the way and get the monkey off your back. This will build a strong foundation for your business and make you a ton of money.

Chapter 5:

LAUNCH!

If you're offered a seat on a rocket ship,
don't ask what seat! Just get on.
—Sheryl Sandberg

Years ago, when I first started selling real estate, no one told me the importance of having a personal database of contacts—people you know and are acquainted with— and quite frankly, I didn't want a list of the people I knew and were acquainted with! You see, I lived in the Atlanta suburbs surrounded by friends and family that had always seen me as, shall we say, a free spirit. I never stuck with a career for long. I'd like to think it's because I had, and still have, an entrepreneurial spirit, which to them simply meant I was unemployed and struggling.

In their opinion, getting licensed and selling real estate was just another job in a long line of opportunities I'd had with very little to show for it, so I was embarrassed and a little scared, and I wanted to prove myself to them before announcing full out that I was an agent, and I would really appreciate their referrals.

I didn't understand the importance of having a personal database and launching until three years later when one of my husband's family members hired someone else to list and sell their home. By this time, I was selling some homes. I had just over $1 million worth of volume and $30,000 in real estate commission.

Not only was I hurt—I was angry!

"Screw it! I didn't like them anyway," I said, and I stomped off like a two-year-old.

But guess what? It wasn't their fault. I had not earned the right to do business with them. I never talked about my real estate successes at family gatherings, I never communicated through email or postal mail, I was never confident enough to ask them what their plans were for buying, selling, or even investing in real estate, so shame on me! What really bothered me is that I *did* like them, and that's why it hurt when they did business with someone else, but I could only be angry at me. Who knows how much money I lost during those three years, and that's when I vowed not to let it happen again.

Holding back and hiding who you are or what you do never serves anyone, especially not you. How can you help anyone if they don't know what you do? Constantly look for opportunities where you can help and change other people's lives for the better. Get out of your own way, and get out of your head and ego where your fears live. If you want to make *great* money at selling, have a true desire to help other people and have fun while you're doing it.

People need you, and they need you now. They don't want to wait for you to find your confidence, get your fancy website done, or get your listing presentation memorized.

So let's get to it!

It's the largest gap I see in every agent's business. It's either incomplete or ineffective because they never use it. You know what I'm talking about, right? Napkins, business cards, and Post-it® notes are scattered everywhere. Directories and membership lists are laying around your office somewhere, and you would use them if you knew where they were. You have good intentions of putting names in a database or even an Excel spreadsheet, but alas, three years later, they're still sitting on scraps of paper on your desk collecting dust or crammed in a drawer.

If you're a new agent, the perfect time to build a database is in the first few weeks of your career while you're getting licensed. The reason is because you'll want (and need) to do an agent launch a few months after being licensed, and if you haven't established your database of contacts, you won't have that resource to tap.

If you're an experienced seasoned agent, maybe you feel the need to re-launch your career. By doing an agent launch, you'll be ahead of all the other agents in your marketplace because they've probably never done one. They floundered from the beginning, like most agents do, and they're still floundering. The best way to have a successful agent launch is to have a database of personal contacts. This is a vital resource that you will turn to again and again.

There are seven easy ways to build your database:

1. Go into your Facebook account and private message your local friends and acquaintances, whether you think they want to hear from you or not. Use this message as a template: *"Hi, _____, I'm having a get together/party next*

month and would love for you to come. I'd like to send you an invitation. Can you give me your address, phone number, and email? I really hope you and the family will be able to come!" Notice I didn't tell them it was a client appreciation party or a launch party. It is just a friendly get-together. In other words, they might be missed if they don't attend.

2. Do the same on LinkedIn.

3. Go through the Memory Jogger I've provided below to remind yourself of who you know in those categories. Strive for 500 names minimum. The key here is not to question whether you should add someone to your database. Input everyone you can think of. People you barely know might be your biggest fans!

4. Compile lists of names from homeowner's associations, previous employers, and organizations you belong to.

5. Go through your phone contacts to remind yourself of who you know.

6. Input any business cards you've received whether you remember them or not; maybe they remember you.

7. Ask your family members if they have any contacts you could add.

These seven steps will easily get you 500 contacts if you work at it, and that is a *great* way to launch! If you're new to implementing this process, block off two and a half hours in your daily schedule to work solely on your database over the next few weeks. If you are an experienced agent, add your past clients and vendor partners to this list.

Bonus Tip for Experienced Agents: Don't forget to put every lead you've ever gotten into your database, even if they never responded to your attempts to contact them. They could be from

Open Houses, online leads, or tradeshows. There are so many stories of agents inviting these leads to a get-together and getting a listing and a sale as a result.

 Create Your Database so You Can Launch!
Building a database is always first when it comes to sales, yet many times it's the hardest thing to do.

Create Your Million-Dollar Database with This Memory Jogger

Your closest friends with whom you associate regularly:
- Friends and neighbors
- People you work with
- Church members
- Sunday school class members

People you have been associated with in the past:
- Schoolmates
- Former coworkers
- People in your hometown
- Military cohorts

People you do business with:
- Doctor, lawyer, barber, merchants, grocer
- Gas station attendant, dry cleaner, postal worker
- Beauticians, jewelers, waiters/waitresses

People you know who are in direct sales:
- Business/office machine salespeople
- Insurance salespeople
- Car salespeople

Do you know any people who work in these types of businesses?

Accounting	Acting	Advertising	Aerobics
Air Force	Airline	Alarm Systems	Animal health/ vet
Antiques	Apartment	Architect	Army
Art	Artificial nails	Asphalt	Athletics
Auctioneer	Automobile	Babysitters	Banking
Barber	Baseball	Basketball	Beauty salon
Beepers	Bible school	Bicycles	Blinds
Boats	Bond/stocks	Books	Bookkeeping
Boys Clubs	Broadcasting	Brokers	Builders
Buses	Cable TV	Cameras	Camping
Crafts	Credit union	Daycare	Delivery
Dentists	Dermatologists	Designers	Doctors
Driving range	Dry cleaners	Drywall	Education
Electrician	Engineering	Entertainment	Eye care
Fax equipment	Farming	Film industry	Firefighters
Fishing industry	Florists	Food service	Furniture
Gardens	Gift shops	Girls Clubs	Golfing
Government	Graphic arts	Grocery stores	Gymnastics
Hair care	Handicapped	Handyman	Hardware
Health clubs	Health Insurance	Hearing aids	Helicopters
Hiking	Horses	Hospitals	Hotels
Hunting	Ice cream	Ice skating	Income tax
Insurance	Investments	Janitor	Jewelry
Judo	Karate	Leasing	Libraries
Lighting	Livestock	Loans	Luggage
Lumber	Mail	Management	Manufacturing
Mathematics	Mechanics	Mental health	Miniature golf

Mobile homes	Mortgages	Motels	Motion pictures
Movie theatres	Museums	Music	Mutual funds
Navy	Newspapers	Nurses	Nutrition
Office machines	Office furniture	Oil changes	Optometrists
Orthodontist	Painting	Parking	Parties
Pediatricians	Pedicures	Pensions	Perfume
Personnel	Pest control	Pets	Pharmacies
Phones	Photography	Physician	Pianos
Pizza	Pollution	Pools	Preschools
Printing	Property mgmt.	Psychiatrists	Psychologists
Publishers	Racing	Radio	Railroad
Real estate	Rehabilitation	Religion	Rental agencies
Reporters	Resorts	Rest homes	Restaurants
Roller blading	Roofing	Safety	Sales
Sandblasting	Satellites	School	Screen-printing
Scuba diving	Secretaries	Security	Self-defense
Sewing	Sheetrock	Shoe repair	Siding
Signs	Singing	Skating	Skeet shooting
Skiing	Skin care	Soccer	Social Services
Softball	Software	Spas	Sporting goods
T-shirts	Tailors	Tanning	Salons
Taxes	Teachers	Telecommunications	Telemarketing
Television	Tennis	Theatres	Therapists
Tile layers	Tires	Title companies	Tools
Towing	Townhouses	Training	Transmissions

Trucking	Typesetting	Unions	Universities
Upholstery	Used cars	Vacuum cleaners	Vending
Veterans	Video	Volunteer organizations	Wallpaper
Waste	Watches	Water skiing	Weddings
Wine	Woodworking	Writing	Zoos

Now that you've created a complete list of people you know, you went to school with, or are barely acquainted with, what do you do with it?

You have fun with it!

In the next chapter, we will dive into the Step-by-Step Successful Agent Launch Planner to make sure your business is top of mind with everyone you know, and even those you have never met who are acquaintances, Facebook friends, and LinkedIn connections. An added bonus: this is also the best and most effective way to communicate with the people on your list without sounding salesy or slimy!

Don't take another step without building this database of contacts unless you want to leave thousands of dollars on the table. We recommend a few different database management systems, which you can find on the resource page at karencoffey. com/resources.

Chapter 6:

THE STEP-BY-STEP SUCCESSFUL AGENT LAUNCH PLANNER

The way to get started is to quit talking and begin doing.
—Walt Disney

Launching your business is so much fun! It tells the world you are serious, you are excited, and you would appreciate their support as you begin building and growing your business.

Before you begin your launch or relaunch, make sure you've built your database using whatever method or software works best for you.

Now we will learn how to dominate your database by having an agent launch party, or what I call a client appreciation party.

"But, Karen, I can't give a party. I'm terrible at those kinds of things."

Here are some tips:

- Don't think too much about it. Just do it!
- Don't give yourself too much planning time before the party, or you'll lose steam and won't do it. Six weeks out is plenty of time.

How Do We Launch?

In the old days of real estate, database campaigns consisted of a bunch of emails with nothing personal to engage the contact. This resulted in poor conversion rates and not much more. Friendly emails telling your contacts to set their clocks forward or back twice a year, on the slim chance that this will keep your name foremost in their thoughts, is not a great way to produce results!

This launch planner is proven to give a 7 to 10 percent return in closed transactions based on the number of people in your database. It includes two events, one small gift pickup at your office, and a combination of emails and phone calls. The lead contact frequency averages about once every two weeks so you're not bothering people. Most of us get emails every day from the same people.

Let me show you the numbers.

Let's begin with a conservative number of 300 people in your database. With this number in mind, let's follow the Successful Agent Launch Planner below. After years of experience in my own business, I can say with confidence that you can expect a solid 10 percent conversion of your list to buyers, sellers, or investors. This is where it gets exciting!

Let's use these assumptions for the following example:

- 300 contacts

- Average home sale: $200,000
- Commission rate to you: 3 percent
- 10 percent conversion using the Successful Agent Launch Planner
- 300 contacts x 10 percent conversion = 30 transactions
- $200,000 x 3 percent commission = $6,000 gross commission per transaction
- $6,000 x 30 transactions = $180,000 gross commission after 12 months

Is $180,000 in earned commissions worth spending some time building and communicating with a list of friends, past clients, leads, family members, directories, and acquaintances? Absolutely it is.

Suppose you can only get 100 people into a database. Let's crunch the numbers:

- 100 contacts x 10 percent conversion = 10 transactions
- $200,000 x 3 percent commission = $6,000
- $6,000 x 10 transactions = $60,000 gross commission

Bonus Tip for Experienced Agents: Take your income from last year and add these numbers to it to get a more accurate idea of what your total earnings will be if you implement the Successful Agent Launch Planner. Let's get started right now!

The Step-by-Step Successful Agent Launch Planner
This planner includes my authentic results-oriented email campaign. Follow the following steps now and begin your Launch.

- Set an event date 45 to 60 days ahead maximum, and invite vendors to sponsor your event. Choose a theme. This could be a spring fling, a summer picnic, a fall festival, a cookout, a late autumn bonfire—be creative!

- Private message your local Facebook friends and ask for their email addresses.
- Input/update your database!
- Create and send Eventbrite.com invitations to everyone, including online leads you've never met.
- Mail physical invites to previous clients, friends, and family.
- Create an Event Page on Facebook and invite everyone.
- Call your list to get RSVPs.
- Send out a reminder invite.
- Send a reminder email and keep posting fun stuff about the event on the event page.
- Hold your event day with sponsors, and have activities for people to win prizes!
- Send a thank-you email with video to announce the winners of prizes. Send email and post on Facebook photos of the event. Make sure you let recipients know your gratitude, and maybe share a testimonial of a previous client before announcing the winner. Anything to do with a real estate success that you helped create will make a fantastic story.
- A week or two after the event, email your contacts a referral success story from the party. This will jog their memory to send you referrals.
- Send out an "Agent name (your name) did it again!" email every time you sell a home. Embed a flyer

in email. "Home Sold in Six Days for 99 Percent of Asking Price" (or whatever good statistics you have).

- Call attendees to thank them for coming, and ask how you can help them and their family sell and/or buy a home.
- Next event: Choose an Open House date, and repeat all the steps above.
- Mail home purchase anniversary cards.
- Mail birthday cards to family members.
- Send out market updates about what's happening with housing prices, what's listed, what's been sold, what's pending, and so on.
- Send an ROI letter on buying a rental property or flipping houses for profit.
- Give former clients a small gift each year to pick up at your office, or drop it off in person (book, flag, pie, cupcakes, calendar, whatever).
- Mail handwritten "thinking of you" notes.
- Email success stories.
- "<u>Agent name</u> did it again!" email with embedded flyer

Enjoy the extra income and free time, and above all, have fun!

Combine this system with the other systems that we will explore next, and you *will* have an incredible business!

One more thing: each day, commit to putting all of your new contacts into a spreadsheet or online database. Better yet, pay a high school or college student to do it for you. Chances are you're going to get sidetracked, so it's worth every penny that you pay someone to do this for you, because you stand to make a lot more money when it's done.

Go ahead and choose a date for your first event. Make sure it is at least six weeks from now so that you can take advantage of "touching" your database at least six times.

Once you feel comfortable consistently adding contacts to your database and you've set the date for your event, move on to the next chapter, where you'll learn how to layer on top of this foundation the next money-generating activity! It is a real moneymaker, just like the Million-Dollar-Day Schedule and the Step-by-Step Successful Agent Launch Planner.

If you can discipline yourself to implement these systems, you will gain momentum in a short period of time and make a significant amount of money. After all, this book is called *Making Agents Wealthy*! It's about going after what you're worth and committing to proven systems to make it possible.

In the next chapter, I'm going to share with you some creative ways to find new business and teach you how to easily fill in the lead generation gaps you might be experiencing. We leave no stone unturned when it comes to finding clients.

Chapter 7:

THE ULTIMATE LEAD GENERATION BLUEPRINT

You never run out of money. You only run out of ideas.
—Suzanne Evans

Finding new business is the number one priority in business. Without it, there is no consistency to your income. So many agents have come to me with a sad expression and said, "I don't know why I'm not making any money. I'm working with six buyers, and I have three leads that are going to list eventually. I must be doing something wrong."

They're not doing anything wrong except toying with the same nine leads they've been working on for the last thirty days, trying to get them to do something now even though they aren't ready.

Instead of spinning their wheels waiting for those nine clients to make decisions, the agent should go out and find new business, and build a consistent pipeline of closings by tapping into the market of people who want to buy or sell real estate *now*. They're the ones you need to focus on. You can be the best salesperson on the planet, but you can't make people do something they aren't ready to do.

Perhaps you feel stuck in a rut, burned out, or frustrated, and you can't think of new ways to meet people who could be potential clients. Well, problem solved! Let me introduce to you Gene Frederick.

After meeting Gene early on in my real estate career I came to know him as one of the greatest leaders in the real estate industry. His encouragement and insight helped catapult my understanding of real estate early on and I highly recommend you purchase the full version of his book *101 Ways to Lead Generate in Real Estate*. The link can be found at KarenCoffey.com/Resources.

Lead Generation Ideas

1. Announcement letter to all the people in your sphere of influence
2. Handwritten notes
3. "Just sold" calls
4. "We have buyers" call
5. Friends' parties
6. Send out school info
7. Send out sports schedules
8. Send out calendar magnets
9. Market updates
10. Luxury home newsletters
11. Contests

12. Branded items: pens, notepads
13. Important phone numbers magnet
14. Discounts on favorite restaurants
15. Referral postcard
16. Birthday, anniversary, holiday cards
17. Golf course info
18. Boating and waterway info
19. "Get your house ready for market" mailings
20. "Is your home worth more than your neighbors?" mailings

Once you have the full list post it in your office where you'll see it every day. Whenever you feel stuck, and you're not sure who to call, go through the list.

In addition to Gene's great ideas, the following are some of my favorite activities for generating new leads and connecting with my ideal clients. There are too many to list here, but again, these will be a great beginning.

- 55+ communities: Have a luncheon, speak, perhaps have a special guest, get to know the sales rep and the residents.
- Charities: I love giving back to the community, and my favorites are Habitat for Humanity and the local food banks.
- Meet-ups: Join a few or start your own around an activity that you love, meet new local people and invite them to your real estate events.
- Any type of tradeshow: Get a table, collect email addresses or cell numbers and showcase specific properties related to the show, for example:

» Horse shows are great if you live in an equestrian area. Showcase the beautiful horse farms in your area and collect leads.

» Home shows go without saying.

» Senior expos can be amazing if you're showcasing smaller homes and cottages for those who want to downsize.

» Bridal shows attract newlyweds, and they may be the perfect demographic for you to showcase starter homes and fixer uppers.

» Boat shows are fantastic for showcasing waterfront properties. If you have a boat, you need a dock somewhere. Be the specialist that finds it for them.

Another way I love to meet new clients is to connect with the affiliates I work with every day. My goal is to bring them business as much as it is for me to earn their referrals. Here is a sampling of the relationships I like to foster. There are many more, but this will get you started.

- Loan officers
- Builders
- Decorators, organizers, and home stagers
- Any service provider who has anything to do with homes, such as landscapers, plumbers, inspectors, movers, and the list goes on.

As an added bonus, you might want to create your own black book of exceptional vendors and affiliates you work with to give as a gift to prospects and clients. My black book was called Karen Coffey's Black Book of the Best, for the Year _____. It is super simple to create, and clients keep it around forever. Of course it has all of your contact information in it so they can call you when they need your services.

Create a Ninety-Day Marketing Calendar

The key to implementing your Ultimate Lead Generation Blueprint is to stay on track and organized. One way to do that is to create a Ninety-Day Marketing Calendar.

This is a ton of fun because it feels like playing a game. I learned this from one of the most influential online marketers I've ever met. She doesn't use a digital calendar. Instead, she writes everything on a large desk calendar so that she sees it every day, 24/7, as a constant visual reminder. When I was ramping up my business, I knew that I needed to find the best way to leverage my time and my unique personality as a real estate agent. Using her method, I decided to play a game I call the "How many people can I get in front of?" game. I love this idea!

Here's how it works. Instead of just meeting people one on one, or churning the phones and knocking on doors like so many other agents do—and only producing mediocre businesses as a result—I wanted to get in front of people and leverage myself, because there is only one me! Instead of one-to-one marketing, I wanted to do one-to-many marketing.

In the list above, I gave you over 100 ways to get in front of people; some could be one-to-one meetings, and some could be one-to-many meetings. Now let's schedule those in terms of priority.

Book Your Big Rocks First

Dr. Stephen R. Covey spoke about what he called "the big rocks of life." He explained that if we don't do the big rocks of life and business first, we never quite get around to them, and we end up with a less-than-stellar life, unfulfilling relationships, and a mediocre business that earns us just enough to pay the bills and not much more. Here is an often-circulated story about the big rocks in life (original source unknown):

One day this expert was speaking to a group of business students and, to drive home a point, used an illustration I'm sure those students will never forget. After I share it with you, you'll never forget it either. As this man stood in front of the group of high-powered over-achievers, he said, "Okay, time for a quiz." Then he pulled out a one-gallon, wide-mouthed mason jar and set it on a table in front of him. Then he produced about a dozen fist-sized rocks and carefully placed them, one at a time, into the jar.

When the jar was filled to the top and no more rocks would fit inside, he asked, "Is this jar full?"

Everyone in the class said, "Yes."

Then he said, "Really?"

He reached under the table and pulled out a bucket of gravel. Then he dumped some gravel in and shook the jar causing pieces of gravel to work themselves down into the spaces between the big rocks.

Then he smiled and asked the group once more, "Is the jar full?"

By this time, the class was on to him. "Probably not," one of them answered.

"Good!" he replied. And he reached under the table and brought out a bucket of sand. He started dumping the sand in, and it went into all the spaces left between the rocks and the gravel.

Once more he asked the question, "Is this jar full?"

"No!" the class shouted.

Once again, he said, "Good!" Then he grabbed a pitcher of water and poured it into the jar until it was filled to the brim. He looked up at the class.

"What is the point of this illustration?" he asked.

One eager beaver raised his hand and said, "No matter how full your schedule is, if you try really hard, you can always fit some more things into it!"

"Good guess," said the speaker, "but that's not the point of this illustration. It teaches us that if we don't put the big rocks in first, we'll never get them in."

What are the big rocks in your life? Is there a project you want to accomplish? Do you want to spend more time with your loved ones? Do you want to grow your faith, your education, your finances? Are you interested in supporting a worthy cause? Are you feeling a tug in your heart to teach or mentor others? These are the big, important rocks in your life. Remember to put them in first, or you'll never get them in.

The big rocks of our life and business are the most important things that must be done, and if we don't do them, we struggle.

It is imperative in business that you schedule your big rocks first, because that's where you will meet the most people, get the most referrals, and make the most money long term. The following are some examples of the big rocks in business:

Tradeshows/Expos

Examples of these are home shows, senior expos, and horse shows (if you sell equine properties). You will typically have an opportunity to meet between 200 and 500 people at these events.

Client Appreciation Parties

Invite every person you've ever met in your life—friends, family, neighbors, leads, college and high school acquaintances—everyone! You may be thinking, *I don't have very many former clients. How can I have this event?* Your attendees don't know if you had two clients last year or 200. Do it anyway.

Speaking Opportunities

Perhaps one of your skills is public speaking. If so, get in front of others and share relevant information about the housing market, how to buy a home, how to increase the equity in the home you have—any topic that shows you're a leader in your field. Find some venues where you can share your expertise. Some examples are Rotary Club meetings, first-time homebuyer seminars, and library discussion groups.

Sponsorships

Another big rock could be sponsoring sports teams, but this can be a waste of time and money if you don't have a thorough follow-up system in place. Many organizations expect you to sponsor their team or organization for an entire year. Before you do this, make sure you're getting everything you need to make it a successful venture. For example, will you have access to an email list of everyone in the organization? If so, are you allowed to reach out to them? Will you have the freedom to host a get-together for the organization's members or speak at one of their events?

Sponsorship only pays off if you can connect with the people in that organization in a way that's relevant to your business. You can't just put money toward sponsorship, get your logo on a t-shirt, and expect people to bring you business. It doesn't work that way. You need to be able to communicate with the members and follow up afterward if you want a sponsorship opportunity to be successful.

Add Your Monthly Rocks

Now that you've filled your calendar with the big rocks, which typically happen once a year or once a quarter, fill in your monthly rocks.

Open Houses Every Two Weeks

You may have heard the saying "Open Houses don't sell houses," and that is 100 percent correct, unless you do them with an extraordinary high level of skill and intention. A strategy we ask our clients to implement is called the Six-Figure Open House Strategy. The idea behind it is to do an Open House every other weekend in such a way that it brings in a minimum of $100,000 in commissions to you long term. Right now, however, I want you to schedule Open House events every two weeks for the next ninety days and commit to finding those houses and holding the events.

Add Your Daily Rocks

Next, let's work on your daily rocks. As part of the Ultimate Lead Generation Blueprint, it's important to do daily activities that keep your pipeline filled with new business. The following are a few examples of that, but don't forget to go back to your list of 100+ ideas if you're running out of steam:

- FSBO system
- Expired listings system
- Sphere of influence contacts
- Circle prospecting
- Probate leads
- Divorce leads
- Effective networking

Online Lead Generation

Online leads have their place. They can be fun and exciting, but they can also be extremely expensive if you don't know how to convert them. If you want to grow, leverage, and scale your business to be as big as possible, take advantage of all the online lead generation tools available.

Here are just a few websites where you can get leads:

- Realtor.com
- Facebook ads
- Zillow.com
- Google pay-per-click ads
- Commissions, Inc.
- Kunversion
- Zurple

For Sale by Owners and Expired Listings

For Sale by Owners and Expired Listings are an age-old source of leads that can be extremely lucrative, but agents all over North America seem to beat them to death with cold calls and door-knocking tactics that have given real estate agents a horribly bad reputation. Chasing and many times harassing these leads is embarrassing to the rest of the professionals in our industry. It doesn't mean you can't contact them, but please earn the right to do so. My suggestion is to find an agent, coach, or mentor skilled in this area, one that doesn't chase, doesn't sound fake and salesy, and is professional in the way they approach these leads.

If you implement everything that we have discussed in this book so far:

- Create a winning mindset with your One Page.

- Experience daily success by following your Million-Dollar-Day Schedule.
- Build a strong foundation with a database of contacts, and launch with success.
- Schedule your big rocks such as the FSBO/expired listing strategies and events.
- Enhance your skills with conversations that convert into listings and sales.
- Hire a part-time assistant to make calls and create extreme accountability for you, even before you think you need an assistant.

Your calendar will look like this:

2 client appreciation events for database each year with 50 attendees = 5-10 closings per year

4 tradeshows/expos each year = 8-10 closings per year

2 Six-Figure Open Houses each month for 12 months = 24-36 closings per year

FSBO/Expired system (depends on your market) = approximately 4 listings per month = 3 sales = 24-36 closings per year

61-92 total closings

Now comes the exciting part. Let me show you in real money what these consistent activities will produce.

According to the National Association of Realtors, the average home sale price in the United States is $200,000.

The average commission that real estate agents earn across the United States is 2.75 percent, which means $5,500 gross commission per transaction on the sale of a $200,000 home.

Let's do the math!

61-92 closings per year = $335,500 – $506,000 gross commission.

Not too bad, right? That's gross earnings, not net, so let's subtract some typical expenses:

- Commission split with your broker
- Taxes
- Mailings, marketing, and advertising
- Cost of client appreciation parties
- Printing and supplies
- Closing gifts
- Part-time administrative help

Even with these expenses, you've still earned *half a million dollars* in half the time it would normally take you to earn this amount, and it was totally achievable because you followed a proven system.

Now, let's bring it down to everyday reality. What gets in your way of accomplishing this goal? Do any of these resonate with you?

- Lack of a schedule
- Lack of discipline
- Feeling overwhelmed
- No accountability and insufficient focus
- Ineffective skills
- Lack of confidence

- Negative mindset
- Laziness
- The need for improvement in leadership skills
- Lack of purpose
- Insufficient understanding of how to approach real estate sales like a business rather than a hobby

You might have experienced these in your own business, but none of these things should get in your way. When they pop up, and they will, refocus your efforts on the skills, methods, and systems in this book. Plan your work and work your plan. Be consistent.

No one becomes an overnight success in real estate sales. It takes consistent, focused effort and determination. Making this kind of money is possible, but it's not easy. You need skill, motivation, resourcefulness, guidance, and hard work.

Are there any reasons why you can't accomplish these things? Think about your personal life and your business as they are right now. Are there any people, activities, and habits you need to eliminate? Are there any areas of wasteful spending you can eliminate so you can put more money into growing your business?

Do whatever is necessary to create an environment of success. Cut negativity out of your life, remove gossip from your conversations, and strive to speak only the positive. Walk away from anyone or anything that drags you down and diminishes your physical health, spiritual growth, or emotional stability.

Chapter 8:

GETTING RESULTS FROM YOUR SIGNATURE SUCCESS SELLING SYSTEM

You wouldn't worry so much about what others think of you if you realized how seldom they do.
—Eleanor Roosevelt

D o you ever get the feeling that buyers and sellers don't want to do business with you? Why do you think that is? I know all about that. Six months into the real estate business, and not one transaction closed—that was my reality! I had nothing in the pipeline, and I was ready to give up and get a nine-to-five job in a drab cubicle with a boss looking over my shoulder.

I had to figure this out and fast.

I was making the calls, knocking on doors, emailing regularly, even tap dancing on their front lawn to get their attention (not really), but nothing was happening!

What I realized was that for all the tap dancing I did, buyers and sellers had no frame of reference about who I was or why they should hire me. They didn't know me, like me, or trust me. In an industry of more than 1.2 million real estate agents across the United States, I realized I had to do something very different, if not downright amazing. I had to stand out and somehow position myself to be the agent they *had* to have.

So, I asked myself some honest questions:

- What do I need to know so that sellers and buyers will feel comfortable and excited about working with an agent they have never met?
- What results do my clients want?
- Do the homeowners want a new friend, or do they want someone who will sell their home for the listing price or better?
- Do the buyers want an agent who knows only as much as they can find online, or do they want an agent who can find homes that haven't even hit the MLS yet?

Then, I did some research, asked the advice of experienced, successful agents, and created a list of results I wanted to achieve and the steps needed to make that happen.

What I discovered is that my results-oriented marketing plus signature steps turned out to be a highly converting pre-listing packet for sellers and a pre-buyer packet for buyers.

Wow! Could this be it?

I created a sixteen-page packet that answered the most common questions prospective sellers ask. I printed it in full color, spiral-bound it, and placed it in a white envelope. I wanted to be different, so no yellow envelope for me! Before stuffing those envelopes, I put them in the printer, opened the Word doc of my best success story, and printed that on the backs of the envelopes.

If I spoke to someone and they told me they were even remotely interested in listing their home with a real estate agent or buying a new home, I sent them the packet. I waited three days after they received it, and then I called to follow up:

- Did they receive the packet in the mail?
- Did they have any questions?
- Had their home sold yet?

Then, I set up an appointment to come by and show them how I could net them the sale price they needed to move forward with their lives. If they were a buyer, I set up an appointment to find them the home and location of their dreams. The results were mind blowing! My business turned into a machine.

Here's how a typical day went. I reached out to buyers and sellers, I mailed packets, I made follow-up calls, I got appointments, I listed homes, I sold homes—and made $100,000 in 100 days, and just under half a million for the year—and I did all this in a market that I had never worked in before.

Not rocket science, right?

Online, Open House, sphere of influence, and tradeshow leads were converting like crazy. I had to bring on several buyers' agents to focus on that side of the business while I focused solely on getting listings.

Create Your Signature Selling System

Pre-listing and pre-buyer packets are the most important aspects of an agent's business. They are the secret sauce to getting listings and loyal buyers. They create the perception that you are the expert in your field, the best of the best, head and shoulders above everyone else.

How do you create this perception? By including a signature selling system.

Remember the unique skills you discovered about yourself when you took the DISC assessment. What makes you fantastic to work with? What skills do you have? Maybe you're a wonderful negotiator; perhaps you always go the extra mile; maybe you are the number one networker in your local market.

Here's a super easy way to incorporate the value you bring to your clients into a signature system of your own.

Step 1: Imagine the benefits that the seller gets from working with you. Close your eyes for moment and start visualizing.

Your seller gets to move on with their lives because they don't have to sit week after week waiting for their home to sell. They don't have to put up with real estate agents and "looky-loo" buyers trampling snow, dirt, and sand through their home every day. Your sellers will walk away with more money in their bank accounts because of your marketing efforts to sell their home for as much as possible, and a quick sale means less out of pocket each month in mortgage payments while waiting for their home to sell.

Write down every positive results-oriented outcome you can think of. Fifteen to twenty would be ideal. Stretch your thinking around this and do some creative brainstorming.

Step 2: Now that you know the outcomes you want to accomplish for your clients, write down every step you will take to get those results. Be specific. What do you do first, second, third, and so on? Leave nothing out. Nothing "goes without saying." List every step, from putting a lockbox on the door, to having the sellers write what they loved about the home in a letter to prospective buyers, to getting twenty to thirty people in to see the home the very first week it's listed, and anything else you need to do to accomplish your goal. Most agents never bother with these things, but you do them, and that makes you exceptional. Capitalize on that uniqueness.

Step 3: Review your steps to see if you have forgotten anything. You may want to add some special steps to make your signature system authentically you. Some of mine include getting twenty to thirty people into an Open House the very first weekend, and a wine-and-cheese preview party. Get creative and add your own flair.

Now that you have your signature system, you can use it in your pre-listing and pre-buyer packets!

Here's the full lead conversion process I use with sellers and buyers.

Lead Conversion for Sellers

Let's assume that you talked with a seller, or perhaps you spoke with a For Sale by Owner or expired-listing homeowner, and they said, "Yes, we will eventually list with a real estate agent."

That's when you say, "Great! Let me send you some information on how I get homes *sold*, not just listed!"

Tell the homeowners you will send your pre-listing packet in the mail, and that you will follow up with a phone call after they've had a chance to read through it.

The key components of a successful pre-listing packet are:

- Stats on the average number of days on market for the industry, and your personal stats

- Stats on the average list-to-sale price for your market, and your personal stats
- Details on how much time and money that saves them
- A phenomenal success story that speaks to the specific results you give
- Your Signature System Steps
- Your bio
- A professional photo of you
- A no-risk guarantee at the end

This should get you started in creating your own pre-listing packet!

Lead Conversion for Buyers

You may have heard the well-worn saying among real estate agents that "buyers are liars." What a horrible thing to say, but there is a good reason they say this, even though the statement isn't completely true. Let me give you some background on how that saying has become so commonplace in the industry.

Have you ever had a dream that didn't work out? You wanted this dream so badly that you told everyone you knew about it, and then something happened, and the dream fell flat. You didn't exactly know how to tell your friends, your family, and Facebook that it wasn't going to happen, at least not right then, so you went silent on them. You were embarrassed, or perhaps you realized it just wasn't time yet.

Well, the same thing happens to buyers.

They have a dream to own a home. They want it in the best school district, close to their family, and in the $350,000-or-less price range. Then something happens: they lose their job, their spouse leaves them, or they're wounded in an accident and now have massive medical bills. Something happens to turn their dream sideways, and you never hear from them again. They're not lying to you; things have changed in their lives, and their disappointment causes them to go silent on you.

So, as an agent, how do you combat that? How do you choose the buyers who won't do that to you? Hard question to answer? Not really. There's a trick.

It all starts with the first conversation.

Agents completely underestimate the importance of the first conversation with a buyer. Remember, they don't know you, like you, or trust you yet. Sorry, but it's true! There are a hundred more agents out there, all wanting their business. So how will you make a lasting impression, but also attract clients who will not be a disappointment after you put so much effort into reeling them in?

It's hugely important to manage your personal expectations when you work in sales.

For example, when working with a homeowner who wants to sell, you may think you're trying to get a listing appointment so that you can show them your value and how great you are compared to other agents, but it's important to remember, *don't try to get a listing over the phone or even in your first meeting.* Your primary goal is to determine whether you're a good fit for each other. You have no idea whether you can sell their home or what their situation is, so don't assume anything.

The same is true with buyers. You may think your goal is to have them sign a buyer contract with you or go on a home tour. It's not. It's to help them discover what they really want in a home, in their neighborhood, or in the local community; what kind of lifestyle appeals to them, and what their plans are for the future. Your job is to hold their hand through the entire process of finding the perfect home and share with them why you are the perfect person to do that, but first you need to clarify what *they* want.

Ask questions. Be casual. Relax. Leave your salesy scripts at home and actually care about what they need and want. Most agents focus so hard on earning a dollar that they aren't even conscious of what they're saying.

Below is a sample of my buyer lead sheet. You can customize it and make it your own. This will help you stay on track in your conversations with clients. You can download it at karencoffey. com/resources.

Follow it to a T when someone expresses interest in a property, whether from an online lead, an ad, or from seeing a For Sale sign.

Sample Buyer Lead Sheet

CONTACT INFORMATION

Name:

Address:

City:

State:

ZIP:

Phone Number Home:

Work:

Cell:

Email:

CONVERSION QUESTIONS

- "Oh, that is a great home. Everyone is calling in on that one! While I look that information up, tell me, what price range do you feel comfortable with?
- What was it that attracted you to the home?"
- "I will be more than happy to show you the home, but I also have a few other homes I'm thinking of based on your interest in this home. Would you like to see those if they're a fit? (Ask how many beds and baths they need.)"
- "Right now I am logging into the multiple listing service so I can pull up the new listings that meet your criteria. That way when we get together to look at the property, I will have a couple of homes that will also meet your needs. Does that sound good? Great! I'd love to help you buy a home!"
- "Have you just started looking, or have you been looking for a while? Some folks say it's been difficult to find the homes that they like—competing multiple offers, low inventory, etc."

- "So, when do you want to be in your new home? Do you want to start the process then?"
- "Awesome! Let's set up a time to go look at the new properties I've pulled up, and with your permission, I'm going to go ahead and look for homes that aren't even on the market yet so you get first dibs. ☺
- "What would be the best time for us to get together and start the process: weekdays or weekends? Mornings or afternoons? Wonderful. (Get their email and phone number.) Do you know where my office is located? (Provide directions.) I look forward to meeting you there at _____ (provide the agreed-on appointment time), and we'll head out! In the meantime, I'm going to send you some information on how we help our buyers save thousands. I hope you'll take a minute to review it.

Appointment time:

Appointment date:

PROPERTY INFORMATION

Bedrooms:
Lot Size:
N
Price Range:
Special Features:
Bathrooms:
Age:

E:
Area 1:

Style:
Garage:
S
Area 2:

Basement:
Square feet:
Area 3:

Handling Buyer Objections

"I'm not ready to buy just yet."

> *"I understand, it's a big decision, but we have a program designed just for you! It's called our VIP homebuyer program. [Pause.) It walks you through the process of multiple offers and educates you on what you need to know. That way, when the perfect home comes up, you'll beat out all the other buyers and save money and time."*

[Pause.]

> *"You do want to save money and time, right?"*

"I'm just curious about what's on the market."

> *"We get a lot of folks who are just curious. In fact, we've worked with a lot of people in your neighborhood, and we offer a free price opinion for insurance and general knowledge purposes."*

"I'm not ready for that yet."

"*That's fine, take some time to think about it. To help you decide, we can send you some new listings and a packet of information on how we save our clients thousands of dollars. My number and email address will be right at the top.*"

Move the prospect into action:

"*Like I mentioned earlier, here at* _____ *Realty, we have the perfect system for someone in your situation. It is called our VIP homebuyer program where we also have an instant notification system. Here's how it works: I will load your home-buying criteria into our program and send you a daily email with photos of the newest homes on the market that match your criteria. Also, we set up a tour of homes to help you clarify what you do and do not want in a home.*"

[Allow a moment for them to respond.]

"*Yes, it's a really great system. You know how when you look on Zillow and Trulia, or even Realtor. com, and you find the home you love, and it's already under contract, and then you find out that it sold two weeks ago? Well, that will never happen with our VIP system because it updates every two hours to give you the freshest listings of homes for sale. Sound good?*"

[Wait for reply.]

"Great! Why don't we set up a time for you to come by the office, or we can meet at Starbucks. (When you meet up, be sure to take a picture of their driver's licenses and send to broker or a friend for security purposes.) I'll get you into the program right away. When would be the best time to get together and start the process, weekends or weekdays?"

[Wait for reply. Make a note of their preferred time.]

"Sounds good. We'll see you then. Everyone here looks forward to meeting you!"

If the buyer is not ready to come into the office to meet you in person, say,

"No problem! Is it okay for me to send you a packet of information so you can learn how I can save you thousands of dollars on your home purchase?"

[Wait for reply.]

"Great! I'll get that right out to you today in the mail!"

Pre-Buyer Packets That Convert Leads into Sales

So you've had a conversation with a buyer lead, and they've been kind enough to answer your questions. They would like to come into the office to meet you or to look at some homes next week. It's time to send them a pre-buyer packet.

A successful pre-buyer packet has eight components:

- Professional photos of you, your team, and any other marketing photos you have.
- Stats on how many days it takes you to find your buyers the perfect home.
- Stats on how much you typically negotiate off the sale price.
- A detailed analysis of how much time and money that saves them.
- A phenomenal success story that speaks to the specific results you give.
- Your signature system for buyers.
- Your professional bio. Make sure it is well-written, interesting, and engaging.
- A way of qualifying them as an A, B, or C buyer:
  - A. Needs to buy now or they'll be without a home in forty-five days.
  - B. They have some time but would like to be in a home in three to six months.
  - C. They have no idea when they'll be able to buy a home, but they really want to someday.

Since you already have a signature system that shows your value and expertise, and how you get the results you promise your sellers, you just need to focus on your value and expertise on the buyer's side of the transaction, and how you can get them the home they want. You'll want to create a pre-buyer packet that emphasizes total commitment and loyalty in a very un-loyal world.

Visit karencoffey.com/resources to download a sample of my Pre-Buyer Information Packet that makes lead conversion super simple. You can revise it as needed, but this will spark your creativity.

Take the time right now to create your own packets based on your Signature Selling System: your sales stats, your skills, and your expertise, if you haven't already.

Pre-listing and pre-buyer packets are the number one tool to lead conversion. What good are leads if you can't convert them into homebuyers and sellers?

Your packets show your prospective client that you have value, skill, and experience. Take the time to build your own pre-listing and pre-buyer packets, and it will pay off in a huge way.

A Note about Online Lead Conversions

Converting online leads is like nailing Jell-O® to a wall. Leads are slippery because they can be. Shopping for a home behind a computer or phone screen is very comfortable and non-engaging. But, remember this: there is so much free information online that those who take the time to register on your lead capture website are probably serious about buying or selling at some point in the near future.

Many online buyers are "tire kickers," as the saying goes in used car sales. Some are thinking about a dream and need a little push to make it a reality, and others are serious about buying right now. They've been preapproved, their lease is up, or they've sold their current home and need a place to live now, and they don't want to rent while they wait. If they give you a valid email and phone number, they are a serious lead. It is your job to reach out and determine how you can help them.

Tips for online leads:

- Online leads are typically looking to purchase three to six months in the future.
- Try to reach them via phone call within the first five minutes of them registering on your site.

- People typically don't answer their phones if they don't recognize the number, so text them a quick live greeting video of you in your car, parked along the side of the road, going to show some buyers a home.
- If you get a live answer, don't try to build rapport. Get to the point!

Here's a sample script to help you do that:

"Hi, this is _____with _____. I noticed that you registered on our real estate website, and I see where you've been looking at homes in the $_____ price range. Is this the price range you feel most comfortable with?

[Give them time to answer.]

"The reason I ask is because I know of some homes that will be coming on the market next week, and I would love to share them with you. Should I send them to you or an agent you're working with?"

If they are working with an agent, delete their information from your database. Respect that relationship. If they don't have an agent, put them in your database and put them on your follow-up list. Then, send them a couple of new listings that come on the market in your MLS in their price range in the next day or so.

Next, send them your pre-buyer packet!

You can also ask your usual questions of the buyer once you have established whether they are working with another agent: their price range, property features they want, and whether you have their permission to send them new listings that haven't hit the market yet. You have now shown them your value as a realtor who gets things done because you believe your clients are your top priority.

Lead Follow-Up

After you send out your packets, remember to follow up. The fortune is in the follow-up! Without follow-up, your potential clients will assume they don't matter to you, or you're not a very astute realtor, or you're too busy for them, or you just don't care.

I've found over the years that the number one reason agents don't follow up with leads is because they feel they are bothering people and ultimately chasing the lead. If you show them value, your whole mindset shifts, and you realize you're helping them and ultimately serving them at the highest level.

Fortune
is in the Follow Up

Your 9-Word Text

Hey Susie!
Do you still need help with *(buying/selling)* ?
Karen Coffey

These twenty-three words have made my realtor clients thousands of dollars. This simple script can be used as a voicemail, text, or email:

"Hey_____, it's_____ with _____Realty!

Are you still interested in _____ (buying/selling) a home?"

[Let them respond.]

"When can we get together to start the process?"

That's it! That's all you need to say.

I noticed that when I tried to gain rapport over the phone on the follow-up call, it didn't work, but when I used this straight and to-the-point conversation, it usually produced results.

 We've talked a lot about ways to get an appointment in this chapter, but what happens when we actually get one? We'll explore that in the next chapter, but first, before you turn the page, stop reading and do the following:

Make twenty copies each of your pre-buyer and pre-listing packets. It's too easy for this to slip to the back of your mind, and then you'll forget to do it.

Remember, you won't sell real estate if you can't convert a lead. Get your own signature system mapped out following the steps I outlined, and build your own pre-listing and pre-buyer packages that will convert leads into sales. You can do it! Just be you, and your authenticity will shine through.

Chapter 9:

CONVERTING LISTING AND BUYER APPOINTMENTS INTO SALES

The same voice that says "give up" can also
be trained to say "keep going."
—Unknown

Over the years I have come to realize that it's not enough to just show up to an appointment and hope for the best. Anyone can do that. Your mission is to go above and beyond mediocrity! In this chapter, we will discuss some specific things you can do to ease the client's mind and make everything go smoothly. I know all too well the pain of doing this wrong, and I want to spare you that pain.

When I was a new agent, I was grossly underprepared on my first listing appointment. I had a thirty-page beautifully designed presentation that my brokerage gave me, and I was prepared to show it to the homeowners only to realize they had no interest in sitting through a long, drawn-out spiel, what I now jokingly refer to as a dog-and-pony show. They wanted to see a list of the results I could give them, not how many websites my brokerage broadcasted to. Besides, my broker's presentation looked exactly like every other agent's coming through the door hoping to take this listing. After losing out on a good number of great listings, I realized my presentation needed to change, and my process. My charm could only take me so far.

I did a little better on buyer appointments because that was where I was most comfortable in the beginning of my career. After all, I had watched HGTV and seen plenty of shows where you just open the door and see if they like the home.

Well, not so fast—it's not quite that easy. Over time, I learned a few skills to keep buyers focused, comfortable, and educated.

Let's first talk about how to do a stellar listing presentation.

Listing Appointments

My method is very different from most agents' because I don't do a presentation at the listing appointment. I've sent them my pre-listing packet before I arrive at the house. They have probably skimmed through it, seen my successful track record, and read my success stories and background, so there's no need to waste time going through it again. I mention the package and even bring another copy with me in case my original mailing got lost, but I don't need to flip through an iPad or presentation folder with the same information. What I need to do is *sell their home*.

There are twelve steps in this process. Do these steps, and the rest will follow:

1. Have your assistant or another agent in your office confirm your appointment by phone with the sellers.

2. Text when you're five minutes away. Keep it simple: *"I'm five minutes away."* Be on time.

3. After you enter their home, ask if you can set your things on the kitchen table.

4. Take a note pad and walk through the property (with or without them); take notes from a buyer's perspective.

5. Go back to kitchen table with them and ask them the following questions to review their motivation for selling.

   "When do you want to sell by, where will you be moving to, any other factors in your move?"

   "Is your home paid off? How much do you owe?"

   "What happens if your home doesn't sell?"

6. Go over what will happen next at this appointment. Position yourself right up front:

   "Mr. and Mrs. Seller, I want to go over what I'll be sharing with you today. I'll be going over current market values, the likelihood of multiple offers, back-up offers, and other pertinent information. Did you have an opportunity to go over the packet I sent you, which explains how I get homes sold and not just listed? Great, so beyond the stats, here's what I can do for you."

   "We will decide how to price your home so that you can move to _____ [the location they're

moving to) in _____ weeks/months. It usually goes one of three ways:

"You'll decide to price your home based on my recommendation, and I will get it sold in _____ days, perhaps with multiple offers, or

"You might decide to price it higher than that and wait for an offer. When that happens, your home's listing can get stale and shopworn, and your home won't sell. So, if you decide on that direction, I may

"Decide not to take your listing, and it's totally fine either way."

7. Highlight specific ways that you get homes sold using your signature system. Point out what makes you different from the other agents in your area.

8. Go over the Statement of Value/Comparative Market Analysis. Tell them, "I'm going to show you what homes similar to yours sold for, and how many days they were on the market. I want you to put your HGTV hat on and price your home based on the timing of when you want to be in your new home."

9. Handle objections professionally and with skill.

10. Take the listing, or write them a Lost Listing Letter, which is a thank-you note if you didn't get the listing.

11. Implement your signature system.

12. Get it sold!

The more listing appointments you go on, the easier and more natural it will feel. There is skill in positioning yourself with confidence, in a way that says, "No matter what, I'm okay if you don't list with me. I have a standard that says I will not take an overpriced listing. I will not reduce my commission even if the agent down the street said they would." Bottom line, there is a reason people buy luxury cars versus old beat-up jalopies. They want the best, they know quality and value when they see it, and they don't want to conduct business with a sub-par real estate agent. Be a luxury brand!

This kind of confidence gives the impression that you are so good and so in demand that it truly doesn't matter whether they list with you or not, because you have more than enough business coming in, but you hope they will for *their* benefit. This will cause them to realize that if they miss out on listing with you, they're taking a huge gamble, and their house might not sell without your expertise and guidance.

You have to be okay with losing the listing if they aren't able to recognize the value you offer as their agent. It's a lot like getting married. Why would you marry someone who doesn't see your value from the start? No, no, and hell no.

Buyer Appointments

Congratulations! You've converted a buyer lead into meeting you at the office or at a public location so that you can find them a home to purchase.

Here are my twelve steps to getting buyers under contract:

1. Have your assistant or another agent in the office confirm the appointment location and time.
2. Text when you are five minutes away. Keep it simple: *"I'm five minutes away."* Be on time.
3. Meet at the office or a public location so that you can take a photo of their IDs and send to your broker or one of your family members for security purposes.
4. Go over and confirm their must-haves for their new home: fenced yard, waterfront property with a boat dock, pool,

four bedrooms, and so on. Do this to stay on target with what they really want so that you don't waste time showing them homes they would never buy.

5. Review their loan pre-approval. Even better, have *your* lending partner call them as a precautionary backup plan and as a valued second opinion. It's the right thing to do to make sure there are no surprises for them or you.

6. Review the properties you'll be showing them and discuss the very real possibility of competing offers. Explain the decisiveness they will need to demonstrate to get the home they love. Chances are someone else loves that home too.

7. If your state or brokerage requires a Buyer Agency Form to be signed by the buyer, this is the time to get that done. Here's how I frame it: "My brokerage requires that I disclose my agency relationship to you. Today I am representing you and your best interests, which include honesty, fairness, skilled negotiations, and more. If I find you a home today, this states that you're okay with me representing you in the transaction. You can cancel this at any time with a simple email. Are you ready to go look at some homes? Great, just sign here."

8. Never schedule more than ten homes to show your clients because they'll get decision fatigue and feel overwhelmed.

9. Here's a great method I use: After looking at the first two homes, ask your buyer, "Out of those two homes, which did you like best and why?" Throw away the MLS sheet for the one they did not choose. After viewing the third home and every home thereafter, you are asking the same question, comparing two homes at a time, until you have one clear winner at the end of your day.

10. Go back to the winning property and write the offer! If they sleep on it, they won't sleep in it!
11. Emphasize the importance of making their best offer first to ensure they get the home.
12. If you feel it may be a competing offer situation, use an escalation clause. Having your buyers write a "why we love your home" letter to the seller, and having your lender call to affirm that the buyers are approved are great tools to ensure your buyers get the home they want.

There is a science and a strategy behind every step of buyer and listing appointments. Each step positions you as an expert who sells more homes than anyone else in your market. Practice and role-play your listing and buyer presentations, using the twelve steps for each, with a friend or another agent, so that it becomes second nature to you and you're not fumbling with what to say and when to say it.

Now that you're clear on how to conduct the most productive appointments with all the leads you've been able to gather, in the next chapter I'd like to share some strategies with you that will accelerate your results!

Chapter 10:

FIVE STEPS TO ACCELERATE
YOUR RESULTS

n May 1908, an organization was founded called the National Association of Realtors. Its objective was to unite the "men" of real estate and to create a strict code of ethics to which their members would adhere, giving credibility to the industry. It was right about the same time that the Fuller Brush company was founded, the first group of door-to-door salespeople in America who sold brushes and cleaning supplies. Real estate agents of that era thought this sales approach worked brilliantly for Fuller Brush, which had 260 salespeople nationwide its first year, so why not take real estate door to door?

Turns out it worked well for the old boys, but that was 112 years ago. The old-school tactics of door knocking and cold calling are dead. Today, top agents across North America are using very different cutting-edge systems and strategies to not only make incredible money, but make a greater impact in their communities. In this chapter I'd like to share some of these strategies with you.

In a nutshell, the following five steps are for any agent who wants to build a viable, profitable, consistent business without depriving themselves and their family of time, money, and wealth. They will help you accelerate your results and grow your business faster than you ever thought possible.

So, let's dive in!

Step #1: Stop Selling Real Estate

First, stop selling real estate. You must think I've lost my mind! This first step is the key to immediately separating yourself from your competitors, even if they're more well-known than you. If you know how to stop selling real estate, you can literally come into a brand-new market and win every time.

Some of you may just be getting started in real estate, and you may feel as if you've got a ton of competition. Everyone else seems to have a foothold in the market, a bajillion Facebook followers, and a bunch of people reading their slick newsletter every month, and you're sitting there thinking, *Wow! How can I even remotely compete with that?*

Well, here's how. When someone asks you "What do you do?" how do you reply? How do you answer that question? Think about that for a second.

If you say, "I'm a Realtor," or "I'm a real estate agent," or anything remotely like that, you are leaving tens of thousands of dollars on the table every month! Saying "Well, I have these four designations, my company is XYZ, and we have a 21-point marketing plan" is the absolute wrong thing to say.

Listen to me. If you don't get clear on what you're selling, and how to answer that question, you're leaving lots of money on the table just by presenting yourself the wrong way.

Write the following on a sticky note and put it in your office:

Customers and potential clients don't care about real estate. They don't care about the work I do. They don't care how many designations I have. They don't care about what company I work for, or what top percent of my company I'm in. They only care about the result I can help them achieve.

This is something very few agents really understand. The only thing your clients care about is the outcome you can give them. They don't care about how many websites you IDX feed to. They only care about what matters to them: the result.

Until you understand that, it's impossible to get the clients that you want at the commission that you want, any time you want. But once you get this first step, you immediately catapult yourself way ahead of all of your competitors, because chances are they don't get it either, and they're not going to get it.

Let me ask you: what is the most powerful, awesome, incredible outcome you can provide for your client? Answer that question right now. Then build 100 percent of your communication around that answer.

For example, when someone asks, "Oh, what do you do?" and you answer, "Well, I'm a Realtor," you're not talking about the outcome.

Instead, answer like this:

"What do you do?"

"Well, I help people who are looking to sell their home list and sell it in a matter of days, not weeks. And usually I can do it for 100 percent or more of the asking price."

Think about it. If I run into you at a convention, I ask you that question, and I'm thinking of selling my home, what do you think I will say?

"Oh, my God! I'm thinking about selling my home! How can we work together? That's exactly what I need!"

Every single time one of my agents talks to someone in the market and answers that question in terms of the outcome, that person turns around and says, "How can we work together?"

Don't talk about your 21-point marketing plan; don't talk about how great you are or how great your company is. Instead, talk about the outcome you create for people. When you do, you're going to realize that's really all anyone cares about, and all of this other stuff you've been saying for so many years is just crazy.

Bottom line: Stop selling real estate, and sell the results your clients want. From your very first interaction, show your prospects, beyond any shadow of a doubt, that you are the best of the best and what they want, you have.

If you don't change this one step in your business, you're always going to be struggling. Your clients will always be walking over you, disrespecting your time and your boundaries. But once you understand it and really grasp it, it changes everything!

Step #2: Charge What You're Worth

The second step to accelerating your results is charging what you're worth. Now that you know your outcome from step #1—such as selling homes in days, or saving buyers thousands on their dream home—the next question you should be asking yourself is, "What is that outcome worth?"

What is it worth to get the best price possible for your seller? What is it worth to have their home not sit on the market for months? What is it worth to get twenty to thirty people into the seller's home the very first week it's on the market? What is it worth to reunite a family who is separated?

Personally, I believe those things are priceless. If that's the case, why are you cutting your commissions? Why are you charging what your competitors are charging? These outcomes are about quality of life, and they are priceless—and you have great value.

It's not until you understand your value that you have the strength and the stance to charge the commission you're worth. The outcomes you provide for your clients—the service and the experience they get to have by working with you—are worth every single penny and more. The more, of course, is 7 percent and 8 percent commission rates. You absolutely need to be charging a minimum of 6 percent, but never less than 6 percent.

So, why aren't you?

There are only three possible reasons you're not charging what you're worth:

1. You don't believe you're worth that much.
2. You do believe you're worth that much, but you think nobody is going to pay it.
3. You believe the high prices might hurt your clients.

We already talked about the first reason. I hope you now understand you're creating a massive outcome for your client. You're solving a major life challenge. So, you *are* worth every penny of a 6 percent and 7 percent commission. The moment you take that stance and say good-bye to someone who is not a good fit for you, your business is going to soar.

Now let's talk about the second reason: believing no one will pay it. The truth is that high prices reassure your clients they are buying the best. There's a reason people shop at Nordstrom:

buying the best feels really good. There's a reason people drive Mercedes: again, buying the best feels really good.

Your prospect wants to feel really good! When we have a real problem, something we absolutely need to fix and we're serious about fixing, do we bargain hunt? No, we don't! We want the best solution out there.

If you were on the verge of divorce, would you go to the budget counselor down the street charging $15 an hour for marriage counseling? You wouldn't if you wanted to save your marriage. You would hire the best.

My agents and I have found that charging those higher prices causes people to automatically feel you are the best. They'll believe you're occupying a power position in the market, and that's what you want. So, they will pay it.

Finally, let's talk about the third reason. In depressed areas, you might think charging a high commission for what you do will hurt your clients, because maybe the folks are upside down in their mortgage. But when you start charging a premium, you're going to find that people become resourceful. Your clients will immediately start doing what you say, and they will start treating you with respect.

The best reason to charge what you're worth is that your clients become much easier to work with! Why is that? You start attracting the committed.

Here's the bottom line. *Don't base your commission on what your competition is doing, because they're irrelevant.* Why should someone else's limitations affect yours? Be strong. Set your prices based on what it's worth to have the outcome you provide.

Step #3: Create a Lead-Converting Machine

As you learned in chapter 7, there are a hundred ways from Sunday to generate leads. You can get leads from Zillow, Realtor. com, Commissions Inc., Facebook, Instagram, and any number of different websites. Leads are easy to come by. But if you don't know how to convert them, you're pretty much broke.

In chapters 8 and 9, you learned how to convert your leads effectively. However, when you start generating a lot of leads, it's time to create a lead-converting machine.

If you're spending your personal time generating and converting every lead, your income is limited, because you can only talk to so many prospective clients one on one. Your freedom is limited, because you're spending all day chasing leads. And your impact is limited, because there are only so many hours in the day.

If you really want to accelerate your results and get out of the place where you're working eighty hours a week making five to ten thousand dollars a month, you're going to have to do things differently. If you've been in this industry for any length of time, you will have noticed that when most agents zig, you have to learn to zag. You definitely don't want to be doing the same things everyone else is doing.

There are people out there right now, today, who need your help. They are suffering without your help. Think of the expired who can't sell their home, or the couple who can't pay their mortgage. What about the woman who is getting a divorce, or the family who has just lost a loved one and needs to sell the family home? What about the father who lost his job and is losing everything? Those suffering people don't have time to wait for you to get your website up and running, to brand yourself, to farm five neighborhoods, or to have the confidence to get on video. They need your help *today*.

How can you get those clients right now, today, without any of those credibility factors? Here is how everyone wins, and it's a very simple system.

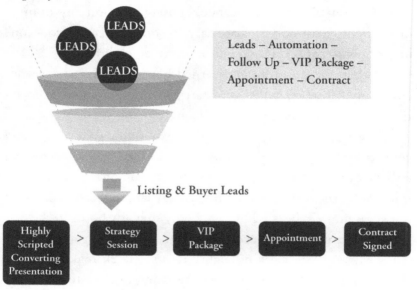

1. You run ads online.
2. People click on the ads.
3. They are sent to a presentation, and on that presentation, you offer the chance to get on the phone with you.
4. They make the appointment.
5. You send them your special VIP package (i.e., the Signature Selling System packet you created in chapter 8) before the appointment, so that they fall in love with you before you ever get there.
6. You go on an appointment with them, and you sign them as a client.

That's it. My work here is done. Doesn't that seem a lot simpler than doing all that other stuff and taking years to figure it out? It's just six steps!

Your leads move from an online ad to an automated presentation. Notice the word *automated*; no one is having to cold call or door knock. That is heaven in the real estate industry, and as women, we don't want to be chasing those leads; we want them to automatically come to us. Attraction.

How the Lead-Converting Machine Works

Let's break it down. Online leads come from many different places, but mainly Facebook and Instagram. Immediately, when they click on the ad, they are sent to a landing page where they see an automated presentation, which will be highly scripted and highly converting.

Your online ad and presentation run 24/7, which means even if they see your ad at midnight, they can click on it and receive an automated presentation they can watch immediately. At any time of day or night, your ad and presentation are creating warm, amazing connections between you and your prospects, which invites them to reach out to you. And it also establishes you as an authority.

Strategy Session

This funnel is then going to move your lead from the presentation to a strategy call with you. From here, you can generally follow the process you learned in chapters 8 and 9. The strategy call should last about fifteen to twenty minutes, and your goal is to schedule an in-person listing appointment.

For the strategy call, you're going to get on the phone and pre-qualify them. Ask questions, speak about results and outcomes, and then invite them to make a full listing appointment with you, where you will create a strategy for how to sell their home. Even if they're three, six, or nine months out from selling or buying, you'll be first in line to list them.

VIP Package

Once you've spoken to them on the phone and schedule an actual listing appointment, here is what you will say.

"Great! I'll meet you Saturday at 10:00 a.m. In the meantime, I'm going to send you my VIP package. I hope you'll take a minute to review it before I arrive on Saturday."

Can you see how we are upleveling the customer experience?

The VIP package establishes your authority. It's positioning you as a professional and an expert. It shares your results and has nothing to do with ego. The package is all about the results you provide.

Tip: You can hire a part-time admin or family member for minimum wage to send out the packages and confirm appointments. You don't have to do that yourself. Are you starting to get the hang of this?

The Listing Funnel

Let's look at how the lead-converting machine works with listing leads, such as leads from for sale by owners, expireds, or Facebook and Instagram advertising targeting listing leads.

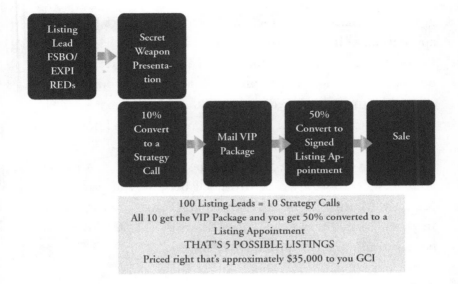

The online leads come into your inbox, and they receive an automated presentation. On average, ten percent of those will convert to a strategy call with you, so that you can pre-qualify them.

During the strategy call, you'll ask questions like "Where are you moving to?" and "When did you want to have your home sold by?" You'll focus on them and their goals, and while still on the call, you're going to schedule a listing appointment with them, where you will come up with a strategy that's going to help them sell their home quickly.

After the strategy call, immediately mail them a VIP package. Fifty percent of those leads will convert to a listing appointment. (For those who don't, keep following up with them)

Let's say you get 100 listing leads per month, which is very realistic if your leads are coming from for sale by owners, expireds, referrals from your sphere, and online. If 10 percent of those leads convert to a strategy call, that's 10 strategy calls. All 10 of them get a VIP package, and then half of those convert to a listing appointment. That results in 5 possible listings.

Now, you are the only one who knows your conversion ratios on taking a listing. When you go on a listing appointment, are you converting to a signed contract 80 percent of the time? Fifty percent? Remember, these leads are people who don't know you, so your conversion rate will be somewhere between 50 to 80 percent.

Let's say out of those 5 listing appointments, 3 or 4 list with you. Now let's assume 3 of those sell because you priced them perfectly. Multiply those 3 by your market's average commission. In my market, the average commission is $11,600, so those 3 homes would bring in around $35,000.

The Buyer Funnel
Now, let's look at your buyer leads.

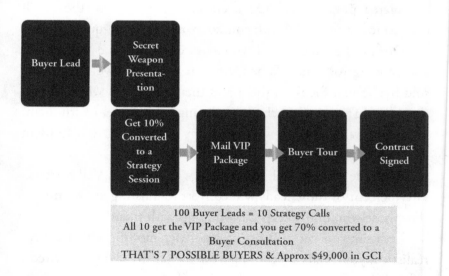

You can get buyer leads from many places: Zillow, Realtor. com, and a thousand other platforms, including online ads. I do have certain ones I absolutely love, but do your research and see which one works best for you in your market.

Once those buyer leads start coming in, they all get an automated presentation from you, just like the listing leads. While other agents are calling, texting, and chasing, you're having an interaction that says, "Hey! Here's my presentation! When you get a chance, take a look at it. If we're a fit to work together, awesome! Book a call with me. If not, no big deal."

So, let's recap:

1. Lead sees online ad.
2. Lead clicks the ad.
3. Lead gets sent a highly converting presentation.
4. Lead schedules a fifteen-minute strategy call with you.
5. Lead receives a VIP package.
6. Lead schedules a buyer consultation appointment with you, which may or may not include a home tour.

Contracts are signed, and you and your client are happy.

Here are the numbers for buyer leads. Let's say you get 100 buyer leads, and 10 percent convert, which results in 10 strategy calls. All 10 of them get your VIP package, and 70 percent of those convert to a buyer consultation and home tour. That results in 7 possible contracts.

Let's say only 4 go under contract: 3 of them flake out on you, and you never hear from them again. That happens, right? Let's say your average co-broke commission is about $6,000. Multiply the 4 buyers by $6,000, and you're looking at roughly $24,000 that month from buyers.

Remember, this is automated income, not a system where you have to be pounding the phones or walking the streets.

Look at the 30-day outcome:

You get 100 listing leads and 100 buyer leads. You get 4 listings. Three of them sell. You get 7 buyers, and 4 of them bought. Again, if $6,000 is your average commission, the 3 listing sales plus 4 buyer sales add up to 7 transactions in 30 days, for a total of $42,000 that month, where you didn't have to grovel and chase your friends to do business with you.

The very first time I implemented this system, I made $0 the first month. I was petrified because it didn't look like it was going to work, but I then realized I had to build a pipeline. The second month, we closed right around $30,000. The third month, we closed just under $66,000.

As you can see, the first month we actually had leads coming in we sold around $30,000. We doubled it the next month, so that was $96,000 to date, and in our next month, we had 16 contracts pending and closed 10 of them for another $60,000 in commissions. That brought our grand total for 100 days to $156,000. And this was in a brand-new market where I knew no one.

The bottom line: a system like this can easily bring in 7 to 17 new clients per month. With this one step, you can and will have more business and leads than you know what to do with.

Now, I know you don't want to be overwhelmed with so many leads that you can't serve them all, and on top of that, what if you want to take time off, go on vacation, or take care of an elderly parent? One of two things can happen. You can either dial back your lead flow and make much less money, or move on to step four and master leverage.

Step #4: Master Leverage

The fourth step to accelerating your results is mastering leverage. Not knowing about leverage, but *mastering it*. You could have a huge database. You could have a bunch of Facebook friends. You could have this gorgeous website, and other things that conventional wisdom tells you that you need, and still not make any money.

Here's my question. Do you want to appear successful, or do you want to *be* successful?

If you want to be successful, pay close attention to this step and master leverage. I believe you need to make an impact now. You should be hitting your income goals *now*. You don't need to spend years and years trying to become popular and then finally charge what you're worth. You can hit your income goals now and worry about your image later. When you get this step right, the magic truly happens, and it happens quickly.

There is only one of you, and you only have so many hours in the day. That's why the first thing you want to leverage is you. You have great talents, you have great skills, but we can't clone you, so we need to duplicate what you do day in and day out. The automated presentation was a start, but let's go further.

You need to learn how to leverage other people effectively. If you can learn how to leverage others, then you'll have more time, have more money, and make a greater impact—and this is when things get exciting!

Luckily for us, we are surrounded by agents who work for free. In other words, we never have to pay them until they sell something. While you're focusing on getting those listings, they're showing homes and getting twenty to thirty people into your listings each week.

It's a machine!

You cannot imagine what it's like to build a massive business through automation and leverage until you do it, and then you'll be saying, "Oh, my gosh! I can go anywhere, anytime I want!

I have time freedom. I have the income that I want. And I am impacting not only my clients' lives, but my agents' lives and my own family's lives."

Doesn't it make more sense to leverage the talent of others instead of spending the next year or two or three trying to build a database, trying to get a Facebook following, or cold calling and door-knocking until you're blue in the face?

Mastering leverage is freedom! It's also extreme accountability, because you are surrounded by others looking to you for direction.

So, how do you begin mastering leverage? You could start by hiring a part-time assistant to work with your database and do some marketing for you each week, while you focus on meetings and appointments.

As the processes we've discussed in this book start bringing you more leads than you can handle, and they will, you focus on taking listings and bring on a couple of buyers agents to tour homes and close deals on the buy side.

Before long, you notice that all of you are closing transactions, and you need more than just a part-time admin. So, you hire a transaction coordinator who takes over your files after the contracts are signed and takes them to the closing table for you.

Wow! Things are really growing, and now there are more listing appointments than you can handle. It may be time to hire a listing assistant who can help you with each of your appointments, or who can independently go on some appointments themselves.

My point is this: you don't have to do everything alone, nor should you. Think about how leverage could fit into your business right now, and how it will create more income, create more free time, and help more clients.

Once you're running this machine and leading a team, you may realize it can be lonely at the top. We just don't know what we don't know. There is nothing wrong with that; it's just a fact. Unless we have studied and mastered something, we have no idea what we are missing. It's like baking a cake: if you leave one ingredient out, it's just not going to turn out very well.

That brings us to step five, where we learn how to do everything seamlessly.

Step #5: Invest in a Mentor

The fifth step to accelerating your results in investing in a mentor. This step is the power behind all of our clients' success: work with the very best mentor you can, and it doesn't have to be me. Everything that we've talked about—getting clear on your results, charging higher prices, building a pipeline, leveraging time—it's all simple. But it's not easy.

Later in the book, you'll read several case studies about agents who successfully used the strategies in this book. All of these men and women are extraordinary people. They work their fannies off! They fight through tears. They fight through frustration. They've done everything they possibly could to achieve their success. So please don't think, "Oh, well, I'm going to read Karen's book, and I'm going to go out there and build a $1,000,000 business, just like that!" It doesn't work that way. You've got to be willing to do the work. It's simple, yes. I can make the process simple to follow, but I can't make it easy. For that, you need guidance.

With so many real estate mentors and coaches out in the market, how do you know who's good, and who's great?

I've hired many mentors over the years, and here are six standards that have served me well in distinguishing between good and great. No one has ever hired a coach just to have a coach. They hire a coach to get a result: to get more income, time, balance, love, health, freedom, and impact. There is no other way to look at it.

So, ask these six questions:

1. **Is this person getting amazing results in their business?** It doesn't make sense to work with someone who isn't getting amazing outcomes for themselves.

2. **Is this person getting those outcomes doing what they teach, or are they just blowing smoke?** Many of today's real estate mentors have never sold real estate, or when they did, they had one good year and somehow that made them an expert. Or some push cold calling, door knocking, and pop-bys, but then you find out they make their money doing online marketing. The best mentors actually make their money using the stuff they teach you.

3. **Are their clients getting amazing results?** Many people are geniuses in their own business, but they can't transmit that power to their clients. And if they can't transmit it to their clients, they can't transmit it to you.

4. **Is this person radically transparent about their numbers?** So many coaches don't share their numbers. It baffles me! People should be totally transparent about the numbers they're producing, so you can tell the difference between who is for real, who is mediocre, and who is great.

5. **Do they have a step-by-step system for fast results?** Just as importantly, is it simple to follow? Because if it's not simple, you're not going to do it.

6. **Do they provide real support and real accountability?** I'm talking about the kind of support and accountability where they don't just say, "Hey, here's how you do it!" and send you on your way, but they actually hold your hand

and walk you through the process, so you can get the same amazing results.

My advice is to ask these questions, find the best mentor available, invest whatever it takes, and get the results you want for your life and your business. Like I said, it doesn't have to be me, but invest in your success *no matter what.*

But if you are interested in learning more about our mentorship program, visit karencoffey.com/getstarted, and I would love to connect with you!

Now that you've received these five results accelerators, it's time to put it all into practice. Several parts and pieces must come together to create a successful and profitable real estate business, and we don't want to forget any of them. We get busy, life happens, and before we know it, we are missing steps; not long after that, our business struggles. In the next chapter, I will help you put together a plan to make sure that doesn't happen to you.

Chapter 11:

YOUR $100K IN 100 DAYS BLUEPRINT AND BUSINESS PLAN

Dreaming, after all, is a form of planning.
—Gloria Steinem

When you're in business for yourself, it's easy to get so caught up in the doing part of your business that you completely overlook the planning part of your business.

You may have heard the statement "working on your business is just as important as working in your business."

Business planning is the second most important thing you can do as a self-employed business owner. (The first? Having the right mindset.) Effective planning keeps your systems on track and keeps the money coming in. As a business owner, it's imperative that you give your business the time it deserves.

Another great saying is, "What you focus on expands."

When you focus on negativity, you get more negativity in your life.

When you focus on gratitude, you get more things in your life to be grateful for.

The same is true for business. When you want more money, more leads, or more conversions, focus on and plan for more money, more leads, and more conversion, and you will have them.

I have a few planning traditions I like to do every year, and the first is called the burning bowl tradition, which I do on New Year's Eve. Bear with me; it may sound strange, but it's powerful. I think of one negative thing in my life and/or my business from the previous year that I would like to rid myself of. It could be a bad habit, a negative employee, an emotion—anything! I write that negative thing on a piece of paper and ask God to take it from me. I really take the time to commit to doing my best not to pick it back up but to let it go. Using a match or lighter, I ignite the small slip of paper then put it in a bowl to burn out. As I watch the smoke waft upward, I say a prayer and imagine that negative thing disappearing from my life forever. I figure God can do a much better job of making it disappear than I can.

I then focus on a positive attribute that I want more of in my life. I think of how my life will be when this is a reality—what will I be doing, how I will feel—and then I write down three actions I will take to make that attribute a reality in my life or my business.

The second tradition I do once a year is to write a prophecy letter to myself. If you've never heard of this or done one in the past, don't skip it...it's amazing! I write myself a letter as if it's one year from now, and I describe what my life looks like then; thus, it's a prophecy letter about my future. This is a really fun way to dream big and think about the future and what you really want in your life. Several years ago, I read an article that cited a study done at a well-known university. The study enlisted hundreds of students to write prophecy letters. When they read them a year later, they realized that 60 percent of what they wrote came true in some form, and 90 percent of the feelings and emotions behind what they desired came about.

So, every year, I take out pen and paper and write a letter of gratitude to God for the upcoming amazing year that I have not yet lived. I start by writing, *Dear God, thank you for the most amazing year of my life.* Then I describe the exact year that I want to live. I seal it in an envelope and don't open it until the next New Year's Eve. It's always enlightening how I should have asked for more or been clearer, and how much of what I wrote came about.

The last step of putting together an amazing life and business is to establish your daily action plan and know your sales numbers. I review my numbers from previous years as part of my plan for the upcoming year. In some odd way, it helps you feel in control of your income. Selling real estate really *is* a numbers game, and if I reach my sales goals, I attain my income goals.

When I first started out in business, I didn't realize the importance of knowing the numbers around lead generation, conversion, sales, and so on. For instance, statistics and industry research prove that ten leads turn into one closed transaction, but that leaves a lot of factors unknown. What type of lead? Am I better than the average agent in converting leads to closings? I knew that if I wanted to grow, expand, or even duplicate in new markets what I had created in previous markets, I needed to know this information and the numbers so well that implementing them was second nature.

Planning can be forgotten and overlooked, but not for long. I believe in the adage that those who fail to plan plan to fail, and so with that I give you some food for thought in the following pages. As you read this, take your time to really absorb this information. Give these numbers the time they deserve. You may be surprised that you are spending way too much money or time in an area that doesn't produce results.

Two things to remember:

1. The real estate business should not be about chasing leads or accumulating phone numbers and emails; it is about results, specifically listing and selling homes, and being a positive influence in our clients' lives as we help them navigate one of the biggest and most important purchases they will ever make. It's also about cashing commission checks that affirm our value and the work we do.

2. The best way to do this successfully is to use the Mindset, Skills, and Systems process that we've learned about in this book.

Let me give you some conversion guidelines from my own experience.

- Online leads convert typically at 2 to 3 percent, so for every 100 online leads you get, you can bank on converting two or three of them to closings.
- About one out of every ten FSBOs and expired leads convert when you are new, and then something glorious

happens! When you get confident, you start converting them at a rate of three or four out of ten. That's great news!

- Referrals: eight out of ten times you'll get them to the closing table.
- Open House leads convert at 5 percent, so if you get ten people into your Open House using my techniques, you'll average one closing if you follow up.
- Sphere of Influence leads convert at a rate of about five closings per year for every fifty people in your database *if* you use my system. If not, you are looking at about one per year.

So here's the answer to the question, How can you earn $100K in 100 days? You take all the systems that I've shared with you, and you stack them together. Much like the layers of a cake, you build a foundation and keep adding layers until you have a beautiful masterpiece. Funny thing about cakes: if you leave one ingredient out, the cake won't rise. It will flop, and the same is true for your business.

All throughout this book I've given you some conversion numbers to play with. Now let's create your own $100K business using each of the following ingredients. If you're a new agent, you won't have any historical numbers to pull from, so the great news is you're able to start fresh with no bad habits to undo and no self-defeating thoughts about how you should have done better. If you are an experienced agent, be sure to write down the facts of where your business was in the past twelve months. No sense sugar-coating it.

I have found that many agents lack the following five elements, all of which are obstacles to their success:

1. They lack a big vision and a big mission.

2. They don't know their numbers.
3. They lack good working habits.
4. They don't have a supportive schedule with boundaries.
5. They don't have business systems that automate.

All of these will be addressed in the following business plan! So let's get started.

Step 1: What's Your Vision?
Write down your vision of one year from now. Go ahead, write down what you want to see happen for yourself in one year from today.

Step 2: Know the Numbers behind Your Vision
Now let's write down the numbers associated with that vision.

What income are you committed to earn one year from now?
_____

What's the average sales price in your area x 3 percent?
_____

Divide your income by the commission earned on average to equal the number of transactions you need for the year. How many transactions will you need to close this year to reach your income goal? _____

Number of transactions for the year divided by 4 quarters = _____closings per quarter

Number of closings each quarter divided by 3 months = _____closings per month

Closings needed per month = _____

Now, let's get real:

_____ x 1.3 contracts written will result in your annual income, because 30 percent of contracts fall out based on national averages.

Remember that number (insert here again): _____

Motivators!

What happens if you don't keep this commitment?

What gets to happen if you do?

Step 3: Review the Previous Year

Take a moment to think about your numbers from last year:

Vacations taken/portions of time off/number of days for the year: _____

Days worked per week on average (be honest): _____

Hours of lead generation per week: _____

Listings taken per month on average: _____

Listings sold for the year: _____

Number of personal buyer sales: _____

Total number of sales from your buyers' agents (if you manage a team): _____

Number of deals that fell through: _____

Total closed transactions for the year: _____

Gross commission income on your tax return: _____

Current listing inventory: _____

Current number of homes under contract: _____

Current number of buyer/broker agreements: _____

Where did your business come from last year? Fill in the number of closed transactions in each category and how much money you spent on each.

	Number of Deals	Money Spent
Past clients		
Sphere of influence		
Expired listings		
For Sale by Owner listings		
Open Houses		
Strategic partner referrals		
Rentals		
Other realtor referrals		
Relocation		
Broker		
Online leads		
Sign calls		
Real estate advertising in print		
Facebook advertising		
Facebook post leads		
Neighborhood farming		
Website		
Investor workshop		
Blog		
Other social media		
Floor time		
Builders		
REO		
Short sales		
Tradeshows/Expos		
Craigslist		
Other		

Based on this exercise, where did most of your business come from the previous year?

What expenses do you think you should cut out next year?

What new areas of lead generation do you want to focus on next year?

Step 4: What Do You Want to Create This Year?

Now let's look forward to what you want to create this year, and get even more specific.

How many vacation days will you take? _____

How many days will you work per week? _____

How many hours of lead generation per week are you committed to doing? _____

How many listings do you want each week? _____

What's the total number of sales you would like? _____

If 50 percent of your sales come from listings, what is the number of listing sales? (Example: if the total number of sales desired is 50, put the number 25 here to denote that 50 percent of your business will come from listings.)_____

If 50 percent are buyer deals, what is the number of buyer deals? _____

What is the total number of sales you want to earn from your buyers' agents (if you manage a team)? _____

Determine your average gross commission and multiply by your total number of sales goal to determine your gross commission income: _____

Where would you like your business to come from this year? Note: You'll notice that some categories are not included in this section. I'm not an advocate for activities that don't give a return on investment, so I've removed them so you're not tempted to do them.

	Number of Deals	Money Spent
Past clients		
Sphere of influence		
Expired listings		
For Sale by Owner listings		
Open houses		
Events		
Tradeshows/Expos		
Circle prospecting (calling homes in the area of homes you've just sold)		
Vendors and strategic partner referrals		
Former realtors		
Staff		
Agent-to-agent referrals		
Relocation		
Sign calls		
Publication advertising		
Facebook		
Online leads		
Investor workshop		
Website		
Other social media		
Floor time		
Builders		
REO		
Short sales		
Craigslist		
Other		

Step 5: Choose Your Systems

Based on your numbers, choose three to five systems from the following list to implement now.

1. Effective FSBO/ Expired Listings strategy
2. Effective lead generation follow up
3. Follow a productive schedule with consistency and discipline (two-and-a-half hours minimum)
4. Focus on building database through events
5. Forms and checklist systems for clients
6. Video and Facebook Lives
7. Hire an assistant or appointment setter
8. Turn on lead generation website such as Cinc
9. Pre-list & pre-buy presentation package
10. Consistent Six-Figure Open House system
11. Find and partner with more strategic partners
12. Investor strategies
13. Start hyper-local Facebook group
14. Create effective marketing and branding
15. Create your VIP Signature System for listings
16. Effective neighborhood farming system
17. Systematic price reductions
18. Look for and hire talent
19. More automation through webinar leads
20. Other: _____

Write down the three to five systems you want to implement and master this year, along with one action step you will do this week to begin implementing it.

System	Action Step

Motivators!

What will happen if you don't implement these systems this year? What gets to happen if you do?

Step 6: Create Your Schedule

To make a consistent income, you need consistent action. What will your weekly schedule look like? Schedule the hours you will work *consistently* to get that consistent income. Transfer this to the calendar system you use, such as Gmail or Outlook. I also recommend that you use my Million-Dollar-Day Schedule.

KAREN Coffey's
MAKING AGENTS
WEALTHY

MONTH _____ YEAR _____

WEEK 1

TIME	SUN	MON	TUE	WED	THU	FRI	SAT
8 AM							
9 AM							
10 AM							
11 AM							
12 PM							
1 PM							
2 PM							
3 PM							
4 PM							
5 PM							
6 PM							

Before 8AM is Your Mindset Routine | After 7PM is Your YOU Time

In addition to creating your weekly schedule, set good daily working habits. Here are the six habits of top producers:

1. Get into the office (or wherever you get your work done)
2. Take a moment to breathe and center before starting your day
3. Ten minutes of motivation
4. Ten minutes of visualization
5. Review your One Page and lead generation plan for the day
6. Make it RAIN!

In the next chapter I cover how to combine these systems in a way that ensures success. We don't always have all the answers, and we weren't built to go it alone, so I'm going to give you some ideas to add jet fuel to your real estate business.

Chapter 12:

WHAT'S NEXT?

Sometimes all it takes is a subtle shift in perspective, an opening of
the mind, an intentional pause and reset, or a new route to start
to see new options and new possibilities.
—Kristin Armstrong

I hope by now you have seen my heart and my passion for helping you become the most successful woman in real estate agent in your market, in your state, and even in your region. I'm always going to tell you like it is and not hold anything back because that's how real breakthroughs happen. But, I would be completely remiss if I didn't tie a bow on these systems and tell you what to do next.

Each of us has a certain set of beliefs about what is possible in this business and in life. We call it our mindset. We all have one, good or bad. You personally have beliefs about how much you can charge for commission. You have beliefs about the best way to get results for your clients, and you have beliefs about what works and doesn't work in your market. You also have what I call quality of ideas. It means we all have ideas, but not all of them are quality, and some are downright horrible. So we can't really trust ourselves to make the right decisions all the time in territory we've never been in.

Perhaps you've always dreamed of making half a million dollars, but you've never done it before. How do you know the right decisions to make to get there? You don't. So, ask yourself, *Am I following a strategy that's actually going to work and will get me to where I want to go in a short amount of time? Or am I following a strategy that's going to take forever, like some of those outdated ideas I've heard about?*

Your beliefs, your mindset, and your strategies all work together to determine what you do every day, often without you even thinking about it. And, what you do determines the outcomes you get, not only in terms of the money you make, but in your happiness.

So you have to be careful to only follow the beliefs and the mindset of experienced mentors who have achieved what you want to achieve, and have earned the kind of money, boots on the ground experience, and commissions that you want to earn.

If you want to change the outcomes you're getting, you have to change three things:

1. Your beliefs about what's possible for you
2. The strategy you use to accomplish that
3. The actions you take to do it

That is the power of mentoring.

As I mentioned in chapter 10, investing in a mentor is one of the most powerful accelerators available.

Let me ask you a question. How much did you earn last month? How happy are you in your business?

If you're not happy with the income you're making, if you're not happy with the clients you're getting or not getting, if you're not happy with the freedom to enjoy your life and your business at the same time, then you need a new mindset. You need a new plan, and you need to take action. You need a mentor to guide you, hold your hand, and hold you accountable to do the work.

It didn't take me long to learn that valuable lesson when my friend Russ drove the point home.

"Look, Karen, it's like this," he said. "Doctors earn an average, in the United States, of about $175,000 a year. And to get there, they train for fourteen years. If you grow your real estate business to just $20K a month, not to mention a possible $100K a month, but just $20K a month, you're making more than most doctors! And, if you're trying to get there without the proper training, you're just being crazy!"

Personally, over the years, I've invested about $200,000 on training and mentoring programs. Some of them were great, and some of them weren't great at all. Every time I invested in them, it was a stretch financially, and every time, it was a big decision.

But I'll tell you, even the programs that weren't very good paid off in one way or another.

The point I'm trying to share with you is this: don't go it alone. Trying to build and scale a real estate business by yourself, and figuring it all out on your own through trial and error is one of the most expensive mistakes you can make and a huge waste of time.

If you want to achieve something great, find someone who has already achieved it and who has already helped other people achieve it. Then, work with that person.

Find the best mentor out there, and spend what it takes to work with them.

We've covered a lot of systems in this book. I've given you some new ideas. I've shown you that it's possible for you to dominate the real estate market even if you're just starting out in a new area. We've talked about charging appropriately and the systems to convert more leads to closed transactions. Once you master all of that, it sets you free to live a life that you love and make all the money you deserve to make.

So now, you have a choice. You can keep doing things the way that you've been doing them. You can sit and wait for new clients to show up, depending on word of mouth, depending on referrals, door knocking, and cold calling.

You can keep blogging every day, grinding out those Facebook posts, grinding out YouTube videos, fighting for everyone's attention, and just hoping that some clients show up.

Or, maybe you're done with all of that, and you want to never have to worry about where your next closing is coming from. You want to make a consistent $20K-plus a month and serve your clients in a way that makes you proud to do the work you do. Maybe you're already there and you're trying to get to $1 million a year. No problem! The next step is the same.

So, whatever you're stuck on, whatever you're struggling with, believe me, my team and I have seen it, and it can be overcome. Whether you work with us as your mentor or you find a better fit with someone else, here's the next step.

Find whatever money it takes to hire the very best mentor in your industry, and hire them. Work side-by-side with them, get your mindset, your systems, and your actions mastered, and there is no end to how big you can build your business, your company, and your life using real estate to do it. Let me give you an example of what a big difference this makes: what used to take me a year to earn in real estate now takes me two weeks! That is not to boast in any way, but to share a vision that can be yours as well.

My testimony is your prophecy letter for next year.

If you want our help, we're happy to help, and if we can't, we'll steer you in the direction of someone who can. The number one core value at my firm is integrity. It's never about a paycheck, and that's obvious once you've worked with us. When it ceases to be about breakthrough and transformation, that is when I'm on the first flight out. I have no interest in coaching another agent just for the sake of coaching them. I am only looking for success stories.

If you're an agent who is not afraid of working, then invest in a mentor so they can keep giving you new ideas and keep you accountable to your own goals. Every day we come up with action plans for agents to help them get started, and we do it for free because we want women to stop chasing business and start attracting the clients that they want to work with.

No two people are the same; no plan is a one-size-fits-all. People are different, and every market has its nuances. Your mentor or coach will have to dig into your business and customize a plan, like the one I've taught in this book, so that it can apply to you and your market, and create some amazing outcomes for you.

But here's the catch: mentoring isn't for everyone. Here's who it *is* for:

- You have to be good at what you do. If you're not good at what you do, no amount of mentoring is going to help.

- You have to hold yourself to the highest standards of integrity, where getting results for your clients is your number one priority.
- You have to be coachable and open to new ideas.

If that's you, invest the money in the best you can afford. You'll get more clarity and more insight into your business, and more closings than you've had in a long time, or ever. The time for a fresh start is now.

Most sales trainers and coaches will tell you it takes three to five years to get a foothold in the real estate industry. I strongly disagree. Why? Because I've seen miracles happen in ninety days, 100 days, even $100,000 made in sixty days. I see it over and over and over again. I want you to have those results, and I don't you to have to wait for them.

Success takes as long as you give it! So don't give it long.

Quick results like these take hustle, grit, a strong mindset, accountability, and the right systems and strategies. You will never know what you can accomplish if you sit still and mull over it. You have to give this *all* you have because the rewards far outweigh the sacrifices. Push yourself when you don't feel like it, show up, stay disciplined, follow your schedule, get a mentor—all of these efforts will make the difference between adding $30,000 to your income next year or $300,000. It's your choice.

You didn't purchase this book to lay it aside and see nothing change in your life and your income. I'm passionate about giving you to you. My passion is to change this industry from one of mediocrity to one of respect and results, and that's exactly what you can do too, every day.

When you implement the systems and consistent actions outlined in this book, you will see an overwhelming number of leads, so many you'll be challenged to keep up with them all. Seriously, that is our clients' number-one struggle—having too much business. How amazing would that be for you? It's going to happen, but if it doesn't happen, you may not be working the system. You may need more consistency and discipline. If so, find the money to hire a mentor who has been where you want to go personally and who knows how to help you get there. Spend whatever money it takes to get some extreme accountability into your life and make things happen. Transform your income!

Now the question is: how will you keep yourself on track and accountable to your commitments? Some agents hire mentors and coaches to assist them with accountability, but that's not the only way. As you've heard from my story, I couldn't afford a coach when I was starting out, so I hired an assistant to sit in my chair for ten hours a week to force me to be productive, to force me to do those things I hated. That's called creating extreme accountability.

Here's another story of extreme accountability: One of the best coaches I ever had asked me to write out a check for $1,000 to my number one competitor, and if I didn't do what I said I was going to do, he would mail it to them.

What? I was horrified! I was already paying him good money to talk to me a couple of times per month, but it turned out to be one of the most effective accountability tools I ever used. Every time I was tempted not to make a set number of appointments that week, I thought about that $1,000 he was going to mail to my competitor, and I got my head straight immediately, and my actions were motivated in a hurry. I had nightmares of the smug look that agent would have on their face when they saw that check with the explanation of why they received it. Ouch!

No one ever hired a coach or mentor just to say they have one; they hire them to achieve the results they have difficulty accomplishing on their own. If you know that you need one, don't let it make your feel less than. Think of it as a smart business decision. We all have coaches and mentors. Everyone needs help at some point in their life, and a good coach or mentor can help you avoid the pitfalls that could derail your success. There is such an amazing life out there just waiting for you. Get ready for it!

You will be working about forty hours a week for the first twelve weeks or so, but then, because you will be so inundated with business, you'll want to leverage some of your time. Money will not be an object for you; deciding what to spend it on will be your new challenge.

 So, implement the systems presented in this book, master them, and expand before you think you are ready to. From where you are sitting it may seem crazy to think you can make $100,000 in 100 days or $500,000 within a year, but from where I'm sitting, and knowing what I know, it's right there for you if you choose it and commit to it. It might seem too challenging, but that's only because you haven't done it before. If you were told to hike up a mountain to stand at the peak, would you want to do it alone if you had never done it before? Or would you want someone who has climbed that mountain hundreds of times, and who knows all the best trails, campsites, shelters, and hidden paths to get you to the peak faster than you ever thought possible?

If you knew there was an ironclad guarantee that you would not fail, what would you do? Would anything be able to stop you? Or would nothing be able to hold you back?

If you think I might be able to help you in your business go to www.karencoffey.com/getstarted

Before I release you to go out there and do it, there is just one more thing I want to share with you: the rest of the story I promised in chapter 1. It's the real secret behind my success, and yours.

Chapter 13:

THE REST OF THE STORY:
BEING A SPIRIT-LED MILLIONAIRE

Aim at heaven and you will get earth thrown in.
Aim at earth and you will get neither.
—C. S. Lewis

After writing this book, I did a long and in-depth search of myself to make sure I hadn't left out anything imperative that would impact your success. As I allowed my thoughts and ideas to percolate, it came to me that I had left out one of the most important things that created my success and fueled every decision I've made ever since. It's what gave me incredible, miraculous results in my business way beyond anything I ever thought I deserved, anything I ever thought I could accomplish, and anything I ever thought possible. I immediately knew I wouldn't be helping you at the highest level if I didn't share everything with you. That would've given you half the story of how you can reach your greatest potential in business and in life. What I'm about to share is private, it is vulnerable, but I'm certain that many of you will want to know the rest of the story of what I briefly shared in chapter 1.

If what I'm about to share transforms one woman, then that's exactly what I want to have happen.

Believe it or not, when you picked up this book, or perhaps it was given to you, something greater was at work, something you may not have been conscious of, and that's divine appointment. While reading this chapter, immerse yourself in a place of open mindedness and willingness to hear something new as I share a bit about my spiritual journey with God and how it transformed my career and my personal life. I'll share the pitfalls, the mistakes, and ultimately the crazy off-the-charts success it brought. I'll only share the things that I feel are most important and that can actually make a difference for you right now.

Strength and power came out of every mistake I made. Every cry I made to God and every fetal position I found myself in stretched across the heavens to create a relationship like I had never experienced before. That close relationship with God is what shaped my decisions and my leadership, which ultimately built million-dollar companies. To put it simply, there is a huge space for God in our businesses. Our relationship with God is not separate from the work we do. That's the number one reason I wanted to share with you the rest of the story, so that you could have the same results. This book is all about results, not just theory and great ideas.

I can help you uncover your skills, and I can teach you mindset, and I can tell you, "Plug this piece into plug A and then add piece B to piece C, and you'll be a huge success," but that's not being 100 percent authentic. The truth is that I did *not* create the success I've had on my own, not even remotely, and it would be disingenuous of me to pretend that I did.

I was brought up going to church every Sunday, and I prayed every night, the same church-going Christian experience that many people have. It wasn't until 2001 that something amazing happened. I was a real estate agent working fifty to sixty hours a week in the Atlanta market, and I was killing it in sales! However, it didn't take long to find out that it was killing me. I bet some of you know what that's like.

As I mentioned in chapter 1, I was having severe chest pains, and thinking *I'm having a heart attack*. I couldn't walk up a flight of stairs without losing my breath. I had tingling in my left arm, and my jaw was hurting, so off to the ER I went just to be told it was my imagination. This went on for weeks, and I wasn't getting better. My body had crashed.

One morning after my husband and son had left the house, I was sitting in the living room feeling miserable and quite sorry for myself. I don't know if you've ever had a moment of yelling at God, but I sure did that morning. It was not one of my most beautiful moments, for sure. I bellowed, "You have *got* to be kidding me! I am sick. I'm miserable. I can't move. I'm only thirty-eight years old!"

I continued shouting at God. "You know what? You're always out there healing everybody else, and you're talking to other people, and you're making things happen. And not once, not once in my life have I ever felt you, heard you, or anything!"

I was angry!

I was in full-blown pity party mode, yelling out in the middle of the living room, when I had a thought. It was a very strong thought, and only two words: *Go write.*

It was a strong thought, but it didn't really get my attention, so I continued crying, praying, having a fit—I was just miserable.

I had a lot of other beefs I needed to talk to God about, so I just let it loose. It felt like I was having a breakdown of some sort, and then the same thought came again, except stronger.

GO WRITE!

By this point, I was really angry and confused. "What? Go right?" I shouted. "Go left? Go write? What are you talking about? What is this?"

Then, when I heard it a third time, it felt like an audible voice. Notice I didn't say it sounded like an audible voice. It did not sound like your voice hitting my eardrum, but it felt like there was a voice inside that said, "Hush. Listen to me. You keep a notebook on your nightstand. Go and get that notebook and write what I have to tell you."

That was pretty bizarre—now, don't think that I'm anything special. I'm not. This is something that everyone has access to, maybe not an audible voice, but what happened next could happen to anyone.

So I got my notebook, grabbed a pen, and started writing. I didn't decide what to write first. I didn't plan anything. I put pen to paper to see what would come out. After I wrote for some time, I realized that I had written what I would eventually call my Letters from God, but this didn't happen all at once. My breakdown day was just the start.

Every day after that, I wrote a paragraph or two, or twenty, and when I paused to read what I had written, I was astounded that it seemed like a letter from God filled of things he wanted to share with me. I was very fortunate in that I got a continual stream of thoughts and words.

The very first letter started with, "Love me, thy beautiful spirit. Your days are long before we meet again. Glory to God this day." And then it continued that day and every day thereafter with a different message. I would just sit down and say, "Holy Spirit, what do you want to share with me today? God, what do you want me to know today?"

From that moment on I had no chest pain. I had no adrenal fatigue. I could breathe, and I had energy to chase my son around. I was completely healed of whatever was going on in my body.

The words, thoughts, and visuals were so loving and wise, much wiser than I could ever be, and they continued for a year. There ended up being a total of 141 letters written and countless notebooks full of questions and answers. "God, what do I do about work? What should I do in this relationship? What decision can I make today that will benefit all those around me?"

During that time I was given many of the effective systems I outlined in this book, one of which was the Million-Dollar-Day Schedule. Whenever I was given an inspired idea or direction, I followed it to a T. That's where the miracle happens, in the follow through. If we don't take a risk and follow through, nothing good happens.

Here is just one example of the miracles that happened in my business at that time. As you may recall, I was working fifty to sixty hours a week when I got ill. My tax return showed that I made $238,000 that year. The next year, when I was writing my Letters from God, I was inspired to only work twenty hours a week. *How am I going to make any money?* I thought, and then one of my letters provided the answer: Leverage everything!

I worked this way for nine months, and everything was working wonderfully when I was once again inspired to take the next three months off. No joke—twenty hours a week and three months off for vacation in the same year, and here's the funny thing: my income for that year was $400 more than the year I worked fifty hours a week and took zero time off. How could that possibly be? The amounts were almost identical. It was as if God was telling me, *See? You can do it your way, or you can do it my way. Either way, you're going to make about the same. But my way is a lot more fun!*

After that happened, I was so excited! I was in love with the Lord, and God was talking to me daily. My life had transformed from high-strung stress to ease and prosperity. I loved sharing the principles I was learning and decided to leave real estate to be a spiritual counselor, coach, and teacher. I began to travel a lot to speak in churches, lead study groups, and write articles. Pretty soon I got a little fame, and along with it I got a little cocky. I'm sad to say that I started doing things my way again, and I stopped listening to God.

Not listening didn't work for me. It may work for other people, but it was a disaster for my life. I didn't stop listening consciously; it happened slowly over time. One day, then two, then a week, and pretty soon a month would go by, and not once during that time did I sit down to write, and if I did write, I didn't follow through.

That was when my life started falling apart. The first thing I did was leave my husband. I could have given you a thousand reasons as to why I thought I was making the right decision, and at the time those reasons made sense. I justified every one of them, and no one was going to convince me otherwise.

Let me tell you, that man didn't do anything wrong. But I thought I was completely in the right and had my reasons to leave. That was only one thing.

Later that same year my mother passed away. Then the real estate market tanked, and I lost my home, my car, and the family farm. Then child support dwindled to nothing, and I woke up one morning a single mother—and we were homeless. It didn't take my son too long to figure out that it might be better to go live with Dad, because Mom was a mess.

Chris was fourteen years old at the time, and the day his father came to pick him up, something much worse than being homeless happened. I realized I no longer had an identity. I was nothing. I wasn't a wife, I wasn't a daughter, I wasn't a mother, and I wasn't a real estate agent. I was nothing but completely alone and broke. My friends would order me pizza because they knew that would feed me for a few days.

When you're that far down, there's only one way to go, and that's up. It was in that moment that I picked myself up once again and cried out to God. "What do I do? I have absolutely nothing to my name."

And he answered. *Go into gratitude. Start making commitments instead of goals. Begin declaring what you want, but don't be attached to how you get it.*

This was when I created the Money Miracles and Breakthroughs One Page. I detached and let God handle it. When I did the One Page each morning, new ideas flowed in along with fresh strategies and inspired actions. I started spending quiet time with God again and began writing all these new ideas down.

I'm going to review the steps of how to do this for you in just a second, but for now, let me point out that the most important thing I did after writing these new ideas down was to follow through. I took the risks, and the payoff was huge.

Have you ever gotten an idea or thought, and you think, *I need to do that!* Time goes by, and you don't follow through. Maybe the idea was absolutely crazy. I have thought some crazy stuff, and said to myself, "I can't do that!" But when I followed through with the idea, a miracle happened.

I was getting great ideas right and left, and they were different from what other agents were doing. Some expanded on systems already being used by real estate agents everywhere. I moved to a new market where I didn't know anyone, and voila, I made $103,000 in just under 100 days. How? I used the systems detailed in this book. The $100K in 100 days system ended up closing out in just a little under half a million in that first year, without a sphere of influence. Things were rolling!

I was building a huge database and getting our online leads sponsored. We actually had three online lead platforms, and I had three lenders, three title people, and various others helping with the cost.

All of these things were going great, but I made a mistake. Yep, I messed up one more time! I'm embarrassed to say I became very emotionally lonely, and I wanted a partner. I didn't feel right being alone. I wanted to be a married woman. I didn't want to be a single woman in her forties. I felt strange being single. My son was still living with his father, and I didn't feel successful unless I had a partner, a spouse to share life with.

I set upon a quest of finding this person, and it didn't take long before I found him and let him move into the number one spot, and I put God in the back seat again. When I did that, I chased after the love of that man for six years trying to fill a hole that was a bottomless pit because God wasn't in it. Six years went by, and

I didn't write one letter from God. I didn't follow my One Page. I didn't follow my Million-Dollar-Day Schedule or any of the other divinely inspired instruction I had gotten. I was just having "fun" with my new partner.

By now you have probably guessed the end of the story before I even tell you. My business tanked. My money disappeared. My focus was gone. I let all of my friendships with women go by the wayside because I was so hyper-focused on him, and for nothing. Each day he told me how ugly I was, how I wasn't worth anything. If I said anything about his negative behavior, he said I was crazy, and quite frankly I thought I was.

I allowed my confidence and self-esteem to be shattered, and I gained thirty pounds. I rarely got dressed and took a shower about every three days. Our intimacy was nonexistent, and I had become a shell of the woman I used to be, the woman who was my true self. The coup de grace was when he said, "You know what? You really suck." I hate that word. "You should just be an Uber driver."

The saddest part of that statement was that I believed him, and that was when I knew something had to change. I thought, *Yeah, you're right. I should just be an Uber driver. Nothing wrong with being an Uber driver*, and I applied. I never had to start that Uber gig, and I'm grateful.

Maybe my story should be from Uber driver to uber millionaire!

It doesn't take me once, twice, or three times to learn something. It seems like I have to get hit over the head quite a few times. I don't know if you're that way. The pain had gotten so great that once again, I had to put God first. Notice that I said I "had" to put God first again, because I knew that the emotional pain would only get worse.

Are you seeing a trend here? Every time I put God first, I earned lots of money and had peace of mind, over and over and over in my life. When God was second, third, or fourth, I had zero money and zero peace of mind. Life was chaos. Everything was crazy.

But there is the gift in all of this. I learned a very valuable lesson that I implement to this day without fail. If you get nothing else from this book, get this! It was the understanding and the knowledge that everything around us—and I do mean *everything*—belongs to God. Everything I receive in life and in business is from God. If I want money to continually flow to me, I have to continually give God what I call a referral fee to say, "Thank you."

If you're like me, you've always been taught that you should tithe, tithe, tithe. Give 10 percent of what you make because it is decreed in the Old Testament. Well, I was having none of it. *That was just a ploy for churches to make money,* I thought. I truly did think that.

Then, I felt as though God spoke to me and said, *I will restore everything that you have lost, your home, your family farm, love in your life, a family, and a bank account to go with it, but you have to know that everything belongs to me. What I give you, just say thank you by giving me a referral fee.*

It was clear God didn't care what church I gave it to, but I knew that I was not to give it to myself or to my family. *What you sow, I will allow you to reap,* I sensed God saying in my spirit. *It's not about the church or the organization. It's about your trust in me. Will you trust me?*

Yes, Lord, I will.

*No, Karen, will you **really** trust me?*

Yes, Lord.

Then you understand that none of this is yours. I will take care of you, and all I want is a ten percent referral fee.

I'm sure you know how referral fees work. It's not that we earn money from the sale, and then we give the referral fee if we have anything left. That's not how it works. The one that gave us the lead takes the referral fee first, and we get what's left.

I'm thinking, *But, Lord, I don't have anything left over to give! I am sucking wind, and it's bad.*

What I realized was whether you think you have it or not, you need to find it, and you need to give it. And understand that somehow, somewhere, the God of your understanding gave you this business, this transaction, this closing, and you need to say thank you *first.*

The great news was it wasn't a 25 percent referral fee. It was only 10 percent!

There's a great book by Andy Stanley called *Fields of Gold.* He pastors a large church north of Atlanta, Georgia, where I lived for more than two decades. He tells a story about some farmers who planted seeds, and every year in the midst of a drought, a windstorm came and took an inch of the topsoil and their seed with it, and no crops grew.

After two or three years of doing this, and seeing no harvest, some of the farmers decided they would just leave what seed they had left in the barn. They were afraid to sow the seed because they knew that the storms would come and take their seeds away, and they wouldn't have a harvest. But what good does seed do in the barn? It guarantees that you will not have a harvest of any kind, not even a small one.

Some farmers didn't plant. They looked at that seed and said, "We pretty much know that we're not going to have a harvest." Other farmers kept sowing what they had a little at a time, and eventually the drought lifted and there was a harvest.

You have to plant the seed first to get the harvest. You have to give the first fruits to move yourself in the mindset of complete trust. You don't have control over any of it anyway, so let go and give so that you can get the harvest. It's not a mindset of, *When I get, I will give*, but rather, *I will give, and when I get, I will be thankful to God.*

So I gave and gave, and nothing really happened, not right away, but within a few months, the floodgates opened, and I mean just unrealistic money miracles that could not have happened otherwise.

When I started giving my referral fee back to God, I also began doing my daily One Page and writing my letters from God. Once again, I had all these new ideas, all these new opportunities, and the floodgates opened.

Soon after that I heard in my spirit, *Karen, you need to get your financial house in order. You've got debt. You have no savings. You don't have retirement funds.* I realized that I knew a lot about finance but had never implemented any of it. I tackled that head on with the writings of Dave Ramsey, and within seven months I was completely debt free and had a healthy bank account.

The cool thing is that all of these new ideas started coming to me again. They just landed in my lap. I listened to my guidance from the letters. I did my daily One Page, and lo and behold, my income doubled within three months. It continued to do that every month for four months until it hit one million in revenue. Then, three months later, I was on track to hit two million for the year, then three million, then four, and the train hasn't stopped yet.

This is why the Rest of the Story is so important. It is, without a doubt, not my own idea, but that which was given to me. I didn't know what to call it then, but now I call it being a spirit-led millionaire.

It's not something that I would tell the average agent. It's not something I would invite a bunch of people over to my house to talk about and say, "Here you go. Here are the five steps to getting all the money or way beyond the money you think you deserve."

But it is something I want to tell *you*. Here are the five steps to becoming a spirit-led millionaire:

1. Write your daily letters from God.

Just write down what you think God would want you to know today, if he could write you the letter. It can simply start with, "You know what, God? Flow through me. What do you want to share with me today?" And just start writing.

You may not have any idea what God wants to say to you today, but maybe you have a question about something. Just write the question and say, "Okay, what's the answer?" If an answer comes to you, write it down. That's the first thing.

2. Do your One Page.

Think about the commitment it represents. Allow yourself to be filled with gratitude. Let go of how the outcomes will happen through the One Command.

Ask God, "What is the one thing you want me to focus on today that will get me the result that I'm looking for?"

Maybe a thought comes to you in reply: *I'm committed to making $250,000 this year*.

Great! Now it's time to ask a more specific question. "What's the one thing I can do, God, to help me get there today?"

You will hear it, feel it, and know it.

3. Write down any ideas that come to you, and follow through.

4. Put God first.

This doesn't mean being hyper-religious. It simply means being able to say, "God, I give you the glory for all that you've given me." Give him that referral. Give him 10 percent, and watch him give you more. By giving him a referral fee, you're saying, "Hey, I get how it works, and I'm not worried." You're trusting in something greater than yourself.

5. Do some sort of financial planning.

I recommend Dave Ramsey's Financial Peace University. It radically changed the foundation of my approach toward money.

I thank you from the bottom of my heart for reading this far and considering all that we've talked about in this book. Set aside some quiet time in your schedule to go over these five things and plan how to implement them in your life starting today. These five practices are the bedrock of my story, and how I have had success in everything I've done from sales to building a multimillion-dollar coaching company specifically for women.

When I wrote this book, I was very clear on how to get you to $100,000 in 100 days, but there was this other half of me saying, "Karen, that's not all. That's not everything, and you're holding back. You're not sharing the real reason behind your success, the real deal of how you got here." That's why I felt it so important to let you know the rest of the story of how it all began, and how you can also take your first steps towards becoming a spirit-led millionaire!

Chapter 14

REAL-LIFE SUCCESS STORIES

And now we take a moment to recognize the beautiful women and men who have inspired all of us at Making Agents Wealthy. Throughout this book, I've shared systems, information, and inspiration, but none of that means anything without the real-life success stories of the clients who followed them. They have done the work, shown up day after day, pushed through the pain and heartache, and created amazing lives and successes for themselves. I love and appreciate them all, and I especially appreciate their willingness to share their journeys. Note: I have chosen to omit their last names to give them privacy, as in the real estate industry, where you are front-facing on social media and other online outlets, there isn't much of that.

They each show us what's possible in our own lives and businesses, so as you read their inspirational stories, notice the similarities between their stories and yours.

―――――――――∞―――――――――

Kelly in Virginia
From 14 to 101 Transactions Per Year

―――――――∞―――――――

After working in education for thirty years, Kelly changed careers in 2015 and got into residential real estate sales, thinking she would be flipping houses. During her first year in business, she sold only 14 homes. During her second and third years, she sold 20, but she knew she could do more and wanted to get to the next level quickly.

To reach her goals, Kelly decided she needed to follow a step-by-step proven system. Being the take-charge type, it took a lot for her to surrender her own ideas and trust our process. She implemented one strategy at the very beginning of her mentorship program with us and generated immediate sales for herself.

That year, she and her group closed the year with 50 closings and a gross commission income of around $300,000.

The following year, she and her group took it to the next level by embracing leverage, bringing on her wonderful partner, and attracting the right group of agents. All Kelly needed was the plan and blueprint for leverage and scaling, and it was plug and play. Empowering her team and helping them succeed became Kelly's new job description, and she totally rocks it.

Last year, Kelly and the group closed out the year with 101 closings and over $600,000 in gross commission income. We are excited to see that she is on track to do 200 closings this year, while still having time for family and friends.

Jessica in New York:
From Burnout to 11 Contracts in 1 Month and Time with Family

Jessica hangs her license in a small real estate company in the suburbs of Long Island, NY. She found her confidence and her real estate stride by implementing the systems in this book and becoming a part of the Making Agents Wealthy family. Before we met, she was working 24/7 as a buyer's agent. As she says, she was "working around the clock," unable to spend time with her two small children and her husband. Jessica was trying to juggle a ton of roles and found herself burned out and seriously stressed every moment. She felt like her business was running her life—she had to do something about it, and fast!

She will tell you that "Karen is much more than just a real estate mentor; she is a 'life changer,'" but quite honestly, Jessica is the one who showed up and did the work. She leaned in and implemented the systems we teach to the point of having 11 pending contracts in her first month of the year. And at a higher-than-average price point, she's looking at amazing paydays. When I interviewed her, she stated, "I had the best year of my real estate career this year, and I win 9 out of 10 times on competing offers for my buyers. In this market of low inventory and 10 offers on each home, that's saying something."

Jessica's success also comes from the mindset practices she adopted. She is happy to share that she feels little stress, works less, spends more time with her family, and has made her well-being a huge priority.

When she began her real estate career, she was a buyer's agent on a team. Now, she is a confident mom and wife who often takes vacations with her family and is proud to call herself a true CEO of her real estate business.

Kristine in the Rocky Mountains:
From Zero to 4 Million in 60 Days as a Brand-New Agent

Kristine Aubut is a driven young woman who lives in the Rocky Mountains. She got her license in March 2020, and after speaking with some seasoned agents in her office, she quickly knew she needed a coach. She had been an investor in real estate for twenty years but never pursued a career in it due to a fear she wouldn't be good enough. So, instead of entering real estate, she spent twenty-five years in the oil and gas industry as a project manager.

Having overcome family tragedy in 2011, when she lost her seventeen-year-old son Zachariah when he was struck by a texting driver, Kristine never gave up and transformed herself through a fresh start in a new career.

When Kristine met with her first brokerage, they told her it would take at least 6 months to sell her first home. Not liking the sound of that, she said, "I don't think I want to do this." She wanted to skip to the part of real estate sales where she got business immediately, and thanks to the systems in this book and her mentorship program with us, she skyrocketed. Kristine's first real estate transaction took only 2 weeks. She didn't stop there, as she quickly went from $0 to $4,000,000 in sales volume in her first 60 days working as an agent, and she hasn't looked back.

Initially, Kristine's goal was 1 or 2 closings a month to make some extra cash, and now she closes 4 to 5 contracts consistently each month. Kristine wants others to know you can rise up from terrible circumstances and overcome anything. Dreams do come true!

Today, Kristine is building a world-class team of agents and implementing automation. I am proud to say that Kristine is still a part of our Making Agents Wealthy family and is creating a real estate empire as the leader of her business in the Rocky Mountains.

Steve in New England:
From $10K to $20K+ Per Month

In 2019, seasoned agent Steve was number 1 in his office of 50 agents, but he had been hitting the same level for the past 3 to 4 years. To get to the next level, he knew he needed to build a team. He had built one before, but it just didn't work out for various reasons. When I met Steve, he was on the hunt for systems that would give him consistent sales and help him build a team, while maintaining the same high level of service he had been providing clients. He was itching to get to the next level and joined our mentorship program. The women fondly dubbed him "one of the few good men." He certainly was.

Steve quickly learned the systems and implemented one strategy that got him a brand-new client in a matter of days. Steve says, "My biggest aha while with Karen is that it's not just about real estate, and it's not just about building relationships and systems; it's that you don't have to do it *alone*." Specifically, Steve learned how to better communicate in such a way that produced results immediately.

Steve comes from a place of compassion, and he highly values giving back to others. While working with my team and me, Steve lost his father, and he tells us the outpouring of love and support from our community made him feel like family and helped him maintain his focus during such a tough time.

Today, Steve has realized his dream of having an amazing team and reaching his target goal of making between $20,000 and $30,000 a month. After Making Agents Wealthy, he is averaging $21,750 per month and is still climbing. Steve is 50 years young and is beginning to plan for retirement. He says, "I can do that with confidence now as the CEO of my real estate business."

Husband and Wife Team in South Florida:
Zero to $50K a Month

Robyn and her husband Claudio, of the Fort Lauderdale, FL, area, were in real estate for 11 years before meeting me and my team. Their career began when Robyn was working a job and Claudio was building his own real estate business. Robyn quickly got jealous of the free time he had and wanted to explore a real estate career with him.

In 2018, they made $300,000 and began to live their dreams. Then, all of a sudden, their business tanked, and they had no idea why. Her husband was ready to find jobs for both of them, and Robyn went into a depression. That's when we found each other, which Robyn says "was the best thing that ever happened to me in my life." That made me smile.

Once we began working together, their lives shifted dramatically. Everything that got them to where they were came into question. They quickly learned our systems could grow their business to levels unimaginable.

They first shifted their niche and marketing, bringing in a whopping $50,000 the next month. To celebrate, they went to Europe.

Robyn and her husband will tell you to trust the process. Don't question, just do. In their first 6 weeks in the program, they went from zero transactions in their pipeline to making more than they had the entire previous year. Robyn says, "In real estate, you will typically have months where you make $80,000, and months where you make nothing, but now we have consistency." Huge congrats to them for re-inventing themselves in a market of more than 40,000 agents.

Danette in Colorado:
Consistent $9K to $18K a Month

When Danette came to us from Colorado, she had been an agent for less than a year. She had focused on chasing down Zillow leads, because she thought that was what you were supposed to do. She did close 4 deals in 4 months, but it nearly killed her with all of the running around showing a crazy number of properties to uncommitted buyers. She had tried other coaching programs, and as she puts it, "They just weren't working. I was tired of being tired and knew it was time for me to find something different to change my life and my business."

Danette quickly learned from us never to chase leads, and that there's never a good time to knock on doors. She committed to implement one of the Making Agents Wealthy systems, which brought her 3 clients right away the very first time she used it. With this initial success, Danette was able to put her fear aside and fully immerse herself in our systems.

The more she learned, the less she wanted to be like the "typical" agent and the more she wanted to be a business owner. Her life changed dramatically when she shifted her mindset from goals to commitment. She committed to building a real estate empire. She is seeing the money and finally seeing the future. She got off the rollercoaster ride of real estate sales and was able to make a consistent $9K to $18K per month in her first year.

Dionne in Canada:
$160K and a Full Month Off

Dionne from Toronto, Canada, had reached a plateau. Frustrated and disenchanted with the real estate industry, she was in survival mode, barely getting by. She would get a deal, get nothing for 2 months, get another deal, and then nothing for 2 more months. This pattern was draining her mentally and emotionally. She was ready for a change in her life and her business.

She found that my Million Dollar Day schedule helped bring consistency to her business while still affording her massive amounts of free time. Dionne stuck to the schedule and added in many of the other systems as well, which helped her overcome the unforeseen challenges of 2020, such as the loss of her mother and the market effects of the global pandemic.

In 2019, Dionne made $86,000. In the first 9 months of 2020, she just about doubled that to make $160,000—in the middle of a global pandemic. Best of all, the systems she learned allowed her to take a full month off to grieve the loss of her mom without worrying about a loss of income.

Once an inconsistent, mentally exhausted agent, Dionne is on her way to earning more money than she ever has in her real estate career, while having time to take care of herself. She truly is the CEO of her own business.

———————— ⟡ ————————

Marsha in Alabama:
New Agent, New Market, $5 Million in First 6 Months

———————— ⟡ ————————

Marsha's story is incredible. When we first met her, she had just made the jump into real estate after battling a rare liver disease for 7 years. Marsha and her husband (whom she has been with since the fifth grade!) had been pastors for 15 years, and to put it in Marsha's words, "they were exhausted." She got her license, moved to a new area, went to one sales meeting, and Covid-19 shut the world down. Marsha literally googled "real estate coaches," because she knew she needed help, and she says, "I was instantly drawn to Karen and her team based on one reference Karen made about God in a video I watched." It was my favorite T.D. Jakes quote: "The problem with you guys is that you've got a 10-gallon dream, but you're carrying a 3-gallon bucket."

In the first 6 months of her real estate career, Marsha didn't know anyone in her new town, didn't know a thing about real estate sales, and was dealing with the quarantine. Meanwhile, she also had back surgery, and she and her husband both had Covid. During this time, they also moved three times due to their new home construction taking longer to complete than expected. If that wasn't enough, shortly after moving into their new home, it was hit by Hurricane Sally, followed by an F2 tornado. Miraculously, only the roof was destroyed, but they found themselves without power for days.

Most people would have given up on their real estate careers during this time, but not Marsha. She stuck to the program and implemented the systems, including the ones found in this book. As a brand-new agent in a brand-new market, Marsha was able to close $5 million in sales volume in her first 6 months, when most experienced agents can't do that in a year. Marsha is currently building teams across state lines and sharing her inspirational story. She is a beautiful example of a woman who has overcome what some would call the impossible and is a true CEO of her real estate business.

Acknowledgments

acknowledge that it has been one heck of a road full of tears and sleepless nights getting to where I find myself now, and I most definitely didn't go through it alone. It may not be popular to thank God in the acknowledgments section of a book, but he is the one that has loved me so completely and deeply; he heard my many prayers and held nothing back. He gave me the desires of my heart and the gifts to transform the lives of others in the most beautiful ways.

I also want to thank the most influential relationship in my life, and that is my relationship with God. I have been blessed beyond anything I could have ever imagined or asked for (Ephesians 3:20). I have been picked up by my bootstraps more times than I can count. My life, and my family's life has been transformed because of his presence. My Father sits on my board of directors and his creative wisdom and guidance is what has brought so many personal and financial blessings to myself and to my companies.

But then I have those people that were placed in my life at the perfect time and place who came together to create one of the most wonderful, meaningful, and joy-filled companies and cultures that anyone could ever want to work for or be around.

I thank Ava Markatos, my Managing Director and my friend, whose wisdom and work ethic and hundreds of late nights helped put us on the map and in front of thousands of women who needed us. You have given tirelessly over the years, and I never could have reached this level without you.

I thank Kelley Tanzola, my Lead Results Coach and friend, for believing in me way back in the beginning when you didn't want to like me. Thank you for walking by my side every step of the way, picking up loose ends, and pitching in whenever and however I needed you to, especially for always answering when Ava texted, "Hey, can you help?"

And thanks to Jennifer "Sparkle" Johnson, my Lead Mindset Coach and friend, who didn't quite know what she was getting into, but boy, when she was in, she gave it 110 percent, and for that I am eternally grateful. You exceed every goal I set for us, and you give back and help our team do the same. What a significant model you are to them and to our clients.

You all inspire me every day to be a better person and a better leader to women all over the world. You love our clients more than anything, and I thank you for loving me.

I most definitely want to thank every client we have ever had the pleasure of working with. It's because of you that I am learning every day how to help more women bust through all the junk that holds them back from truly living an amazing life. Your successes, your strength, and your failures, tears, and hard work have taught us time and time again that what we do works, it is meaningful, and if we stop doing it, no one else is going to do it, and thousands more women will be in pain, going nowhere, without options or choices in their lives. I love all of you.

To Amanda Rooker and Janet Angelo, thank you so much for your hours of trying to make sense of my thoughts, stories, and ideas, editing every line when I was ready to give up. And to Morgan James Publishing, for believing in this project and skillfully bringing my vision to life.

And finally, to Gary, the man who stole my heart the very first time you spoke to me, I am blessed to call you my husband. Thank you for encouraging me to finish this book that was waiting inside of me. You are most definitely God's gift to me, and I love our life together. I love us.

About the Author

Karen Coffey is the owner of a multimillion-dollar business empire comprised of coaching, mentoring and several real estate teams across the US. Her company, Karen Coffey Coaching & Making Agents Wealthy, specializes in working with women in residential real estate sales to create multiple six- and seven-figure real estate businesses without using over done, worn-out systems and "salesy" tactics.

Karen's most recent accomplishments include being an INC 500 recipient, being recognized as one of the fastest growing companies in North America. Along with winning two prestigious Stevie Awards for Fastest Growing Female Owned Company of the Year and Women-Run Workplace of the Year.

Prior to her success, Karen was well versed in struggling. Living as a homeless single Mom, where she and her son found themselves sleeping on friends' basement sofas until she was left a few thousand dollars from a passing relative. With no real opportunity in sight, she decided to get her real estate license in a brand-new market, where she knew no one, and emerged a top producing real estate agent - making just under half a million dollars in her first year. Now she shares the exact steps and tools she used with other women who are committed to taking control of their business and life.

Her passion, and mission of her company, is to help women in business build a machine that gives them thriving financial options and choices in life. A life where they never have to worry about money and being financially stuck again.

Karen and her family live on their farm in the Great Smoky Mountains of East Tennessee.

Additional Resources

I want you to have the very best jumpstart you can get, wherever you are in your business, so I've put my favorite resources for you here. I recommend taking advantage of all of them. You've got one chance to give it your all; don't procrastinate or be complacent. Your time is now, so let's make it happen together!

 The following resources can be found at karencoffey.com/resources.

- Making Agents Wealthy LIVE Event Ticket (worth $2,000). Download your event ticket here, and find out how to activate it so that there is no charge to you.
- 45-minute master class: 5 Steps Our Clients Are Taking to Make as Much as $100K in as Little as $100 Days! This class takes you through the uncommon steps that are foundational to a successful fast start in your real estate launch or relaunch.

- Your Daily One Page, a beautifully designed and downloadable one sheet to remind you each day of what you need to focus on.
- Recorded visualization to accompany the Daily One Page: Take time to breathe and get centered on what you need and want in your business.
- Your Million Dollar Day Schedule, a downloadable pdf to post in your office to remind you what to do each day for the most impact and income.
- 90-Day Countdown Calendar Bonus: It takes 90 days to fill the amazing pipeline we talk about. Sometimes it's hard to stick with it for 90 days, so I created this downloadable 90-Day Countdown Calendar so you can mark off each day for 90 days. Similar to an advent calendar as you count down to Christmas, it's exciting to see your progress.
- *The Death of Door Knocking* e-book: Find out how our agents are super successful without the old-fashioned salesy tactics of door knocking and cold calling. Those activities can work, but they cannot be scaled to the level I want you to go.
- Success stories from our past clients: It's always good to hear how it's worked for others.
- Vendor suggestions: There is a shiny object on every corner in real estate, but don't get sucked into a hole of buying things you don't need. I've included a list of my favorite foundational systems. I can teach you how to build the house, but you need your own tools.
- Women Helping the World 501(c)(3): We love joining with businesswomen around the world to make a global

impact because it gives meaning and purpose to the money we make, and it feels amazing.

- Facebook, Instagram, LinkedIn, and YouTube links
- Information about the Making Agents Wealthy Coaching Program and our Millionaire Agent Alliance one-on-one coaching program with yours truly